Morkies.

The Ultimate Morkie Manual.

Everything you always wanted to know about the Morkie dog.

by

George Hoppendale
Co-Author Asia Moore

1

Copyrighted © 2014
Published by: IMB Publishing

Author: George Hoppendale

Co-Author: Asia Moore - Ask a Dog Whisperer
K-9SuperHeroesDogWhispering.com

Published by: IMB Publishing
All Rights Reserved

Table of Contents

Table of Contents

Table of Contents

Table of Contents

Table of Contents

Table of Contents

Table of Contents

Acknowledgment

Thanks to my dad for bringing me up around animals. I always used to love feeding them all at the farm.

Thanks to my wife and children for letting me write as much as I do.

Thanks to Sarah, my daughter for looking after our Morkie, Daisy. I can see she is a happy dog.

About The Authors

George Hoppendale is an experienced writer and an animal lover. He enjoys writing animal books and advising others how to take care of their animals to give them a happy home.

Asia Moore is a professional Dog Whisperer, Cynologist and Author, living on Vancouver Island, off the west coast of British Columbia, in Canada, who believes that all humans and dogs can live together in harmony.

She and her dog whispering team, which includes an 8-year-old Shih Tzu named Boris, teach dog psychology to humans, to help alleviate problem behaviors that arise between humans and their canine counterparts so that everyone can live a happy and stress-free life together.

Visit Asia and her dog whispering team online at:
www.K-9SuperHeroesDogWhispering.com

Chapter 1: Introduction

The Ultimate Morkie Manual will answer all the questions anyone may have when considering sharing their home with this intelligent hybrid.

A hybrid or *"designer dog"* is a result of breeding two separate purebred canines together, and in the case of the Morkie, this is a combination of the Maltese and the Yorkshire Terrier.

Learn everything there is to know about this breed, from its ancient bloodline origins, to the present day companionship role this feisty little dog enjoys in today's modern world.

Once you've read this Manual, you will have all the information you need in order to make a well-informed decision about whether or not the Morkie is the breed for you.

Chapter 2: The Morkie Hybrid

1. History/Origin of the Breed

The Morkie dog is considered a *"hybrid"* or *"designer dog"* because it is created or designed by breeding two different purebred canines with each other to create a litter of puppies that is a combination or "hybrid" of the two already established pure breeds.

The Morkie is a hybrid that has resulted from breeding the very popular Maltese together with the equally popular Yorkshire Terrier.

In order to have a better understanding of the Morkie, and whether or not this is the dog for you and your family, it will be best to first understand at least the basics about each of the purebred canines that were paired together to create the Morkie.

2. The Maltese Breed

The Maltese is an ancient breed of small dog with a pure white, silky-coat, black nose and brown eyes, categorized as a "toy" breed that descended from dogs in the Central Mediterranean area over 8,000 years ago.

The original Maltese was considerably larger than their modern day ancestors, as they were hunting dogs descended from a Spitz-like dog using miniature spaniel and poodle crosses which were bred for hunting rodents in the marshlands and wooded areas.

Over many centuries, the Maltese became well known as "lap dogs" for the cultured and wealthy aristocracy, gracing the laps of Roman emperors, kings and queens.

In 2012, American Kennel Club registration statistics indicated that the Maltese breed held the #25 position in popularity out of 175 registered purebred dogs.

The Maltese is a single coated dog that is a good choice for people who may be allergic to other breeds, because they are considered to be hypoallergenic because of their little to no shedding qualities.

Dark tear staining often occurs around the eyes of the Maltese, which means that daily cleaning is required and in order to keep their coat in good condition, they will also require regular bathing, daily brushing to prevent matting, and professional grooming at least every six to eight weeks.

Today's Maltese are bred to be a cuddly and affectionate companion dog who loves to spend time with their guardians. This is a lively and playful companion who often retains their playfulness long into old age.

If this breed is not well-socialized, they may become snappy with younger children or those they do not know.

The Maltese breed has a tendency to be an excessive barker and because of this, an Australia wide research project carried out in 2010 indicated that the Maltese earned the troubled award of being Australia's *"most dumped dog"*. Further figures released by the Korean National Veterinary Research and Quarantine Service confirmed these findings by indicating that during just an eight month period in the same year, 1,208 Maltese dogs were abandoned by their owners, making this breed also the most abandoned dog in South Korea.

This sweet, lively and fearless little dog loves people and responds well to positive training methods involving praise, food rewards and playtime.

However, because this breed is very cute, they tend to get their way with their human counterparts who often spoil them to excess and let them rule the roost, which means that they can develop unwanted behavioral problems if the human guardians do not provide proper training and socialization at an early age.

3. The Yorkshire Terrier Breed

The Yorkshire Terrier is another small "toy" breed of terrier whose ancestors originated in Scotland, while the breed was developed during the 19th century in Yorkshire, England.

The Yorkshire Terrier, nicknamed the "Yorkie" was a working dog developed to catch rats in textile mills and factories.

This feisty little terrier was also used in rat baiting - gambling competitions that were a popular blood sport until it was banned, where rats were placed in a pit and bets were placed on how long it would take for a terrier to kill them all.

The original Yorkshire Terrier was also larger than its current ancestors who have long since been bred to conform to a smaller breed standard of an average 7 pounds (3.2 kg)

The Yorkie, when kept in a traditional long, gray, black and tan coat can be very high maintenance, requiring daily brushing or combing to remove tangles and prevent matting.

The coat of the Yorkshire Terrier is typically fine, straight, and silky and also considered by many to be non-shedding and therefore hypoallergenic, which means this breed can also be a good choice for allergy sufferers.

As the Yorkshire Terrier is an intelligent dog that is easy to train, they can be high energy in a small package, and when combined with their natural hunting abilities, this may also mean that they require plenty of physical and mental stimulation, involving long walks as well as games and training so that they do not become bored and develop unwanted behaviors.

The Yorkie also has a reputation for barking a lot, which can make them superior watch dogs who will alert their guardians. If the barking is a problem, when given sufficient exercise and proper training, the barking can be kept to a minimum.

As the Yorkshire Terrier breed does not display the submissive temperament seen in typical lap dogs, they are not typically recommended as a good choice for homes with young children, as they can become snappy and overprotective and because of their feisty temperaments, a Yorkie will not hesitate to protect themselves from rough or inappropriate handling.

2012 American Kennel Club registration statistics indicated that the Yorkshire Terrier ranked #6 in popularity out of 175 registered purebred dogs.

4. The First Morkie

Contrary to popular belief, the *"Morkie"* cross breed is not a new designer hybrid. In fact, they have been around for many years, and fairly recently (5 years ago) they were more commonly referred to as a *"Yorkitese"* or *"Malkie"*.

It is only fairly recently that the name *"Morkie"* has caught on for this hybrid.

Although the Yorkshire Terrier and the Maltese are wonderful small dogs in their own right, many lovers of this toy sized dog will agree that together they make an amazing combination.

These feisty and fearless little dogs that started appearing in the 1990's can take on the characteristics of either breed, in both configuration, color or personality and whichever breed they more closely resemble, they will make for loving little companions.

Chapter 3: Buying a Morkie

1. Locating a Reputable Morkie Breeder

NOTE: this chapter is not about how to breed the Morkie, rather, it is all about how to care for the dog. Therefore, this chapter contains little detail about the actual breeding process.

Although a good breeder cannot guarantee the lifelong health of any puppy, they should easily be able to provide a prospective Morkie guardian with plenty of information about the health of the puppy's parents, and prospective owners should definitely ask the breeder what sort of health tests have been carried out on the parents of a puppy they may be considering purchasing.

For instance, a reputable breeder will have had their breeding dogs tested for hip, thyroid and eye problems, and prospective puppy purchasers should always inquire about possible congenital problems the parents or grandparents of the puppy might have, including any premature deaths.

2. Meet the Parents

Meeting the mother and father of your new Morkie puppy can tell you a great deal about what the temperament and demeanor of your puppy could be when they grow into adulthood.

A Morkie puppy's personality or temperament will be a combination of what they experience in the early days of their environment when they are in the breeder's care, and the genes inherited from both the Yorkshire Terrier and Maltese parents.

Visiting the breeder several times, observing the parents, interacting with the puppies and asking plenty of questions will help you to get a true feeling for the sincerity of the breeder.

The early environment provided by the breeder and the parents of the puppies can have a formative impact on how your puppy will behave as an adult dog.

3. Questions to Ask a Morkie Breeder

Get to know your breeder by asking them why they decided to breed Morkie's and how long they have been breeding.

Ask if the breeder will permit you to visit their facility and will they give you a tour?

Ask if the breeder is familiar with, or worked closely with both parents of the Morkie puppy?
Ask how often the breeder allows the females and males to breed and reproduce?

Ask if the breeder w7ill allow you to see the other dogs in the kennel and observe whether the kennel is clean, well maintained and animal friendly.

Will the breeder permit you to see other adult dogs, or other puppies that the breeder owns, socialize together?

Pay attention to whether the breeder limits the amount of time that you are permitted to handle the Morkie puppies. A reputable breeder will be concerned for the safety and health of all their puppies and will only permit serious buyers to handle the puppies.

Check to find out if the breeder is recognized by your local, state or national breed organization.

a) Medical Questions

Every reputable breeder will certainly ensure that their Morkie puppies have received vaccinations and de-worming specific to the age of the puppies. Always ask the breeder what shots the puppy has received and when it was last de-wormed. Ask for the name of the breeder's veterinarian.

If you discover that the breeder has not carried out any of these procedures or they are unable to tell you when the last shots or de-worming was carried out, look elsewhere.

Also ask to see the breeder's veterinarian report on the health of the puppy you may be interested in purchasing, and if they cannot produce this report, look elsewhere.

b) Temperament Questions

You will want to choose a puppy with a friendly, easy going and congenial temperament and your breeder should be able to help you with your selection.

A good breeder will have noticed personality and temperament traits very early on in their Morkie puppies and should be able to provide a prospective purchaser with valuable insight concerning each puppy's unique personality.

Also ask the breeder about the temperament and personalities of the puppy's parents and if they have socialized the puppies.

Always be certain to ask if the Morkie puppy you are interested in has displayed any signs of aggression or fear, because if this is happening at such an early age, you may experience behavioral troubles when the puppy becomes older.

c) Guarantee Questions

A reputable Morkie breeder will be interested in the lifelong health and well-being of all of their puppies, and good breeders will want you to call them should a problem arise at any time during the life of your Morkie puppy.

A good breeder will also want you to return a puppy or dog to them, if for some reason you are unable to continue to care for it, rather than taking the dog to a shelter or rescue facility.

If the Morkie breeder you are considering does not offer this type of return policy, find one who does, because no ethical breeder would ever permit one of their puppies to end up in a shelter.

d) Return Contract

Reputable breeders offer return contracts. They do this to protect their reputation and to also make sure that a puppy they have sold that might display a genetic defect will not have the opportunity to breed and continue to spread the defect, which could weaken the entire breed.

Breeders also offer return contracts because purchasing a hybrid Morkie puppy can be an expensive proposition, and if you find out that the puppy has a worrisome genetic defect, this could cost you a great deal with respect to unexpected veterinarian care. In such cases, most good breeders offer a return policy, and will be happy to give you another puppy.

e) Testimonials

Ask a Morkie breeder you are considering to provide you with testimonials from some of their previous clients, and then actually contact those people to ask them about their experience with the breeder, and the health and temperament of their Morkie dog.

A good breeder has nothing to hide and will be more than happy to provide you with testimonials because their best recommendation is a happy customer.

f) Breeder Reputation

The Internet can be a valuable resource when researching the reputation of a Morkie breeder. For instance, you will be able to post on most forums discussing breeders to quickly find out what you need to know from those who have first hand experience.

Also, be prepared to answer questions the breeder may have for you, because a reputable breeder will want to ask a prospective purchaser their own questions, so that they can satisfy themselves that you are going to be a good caretaker for their puppy.

First, do your homework about the Morkie breed and then carry out as much research as possible about the specific breeder before making your initial visit to their facility.

The more information you have gathered about the Morkie hybrid, as well as the breeder and the more information the breeder knows about you, the more successful the match will be.

4. Where to Purchase a Puppy in the US

When wondering where to start your search for purchasing a Morkie puppy in the United States, there are several clubs and registries that will be good starting points, including:

- **American Canine Hybrid Club** (ACHC) is a hybrid registry service established in 1969.

- **National Hybrid Registry (NHR)** The NHR is a registry service for dogs from which both parents are verified to be pure bred dogs and eligible to be registered in the National Kennel Club.

- **International Designer Canine Registry®** (IDCR) is the World's Premier Designer Dog Registry and is dedicated exclusively to providing certified registration and pedigree services for all designer breeds. The IDCR also provides a list of registered breeders.

- **Morkie Puppies** are *"an association made up of private Morkie breeders and dog lovers offering only the healthiest*

Morkie puppies for sale from throughout the country. All of these Morkie puppies for sale are raised by our exclusive national network of private Morkie breeders."

5. Where to Purchase a Puppy in the UK

Little Rascals *"takes great pride in being able to breed a varied range of pedigree and designer crossbreed puppies for sale to customers throughout Lincoln and the UK. As specialized licensed dog breeders, we have almost 50 years experience in breeding, so you can be certain that a puppy from us has been given the best possible care and start in life."*

www.littlerascalsuk.com

Designer Dogs - The Kennel Club is a registration and information service to help prospective owners find Kennel Club "assured breeders".

www.thekennelclub.org.uk

You will find more breeders in Australia in the Resources section of this book.

www.petfinder.com is another helpful resource.

6. Average Prices for Morkie Puppies

There is a wide range of *"average"* pricing for the hybrid Morkie, with some adoptions or rescues beginning around $300 (£180) and ranging as high as $2,400 (£1,439) or even more, depending on the particular breeder.

7. Avoiding Puppy Mills

As soon as a new hybrid, mixed breed or *"designer dog"* becomes popular, they also become particularly susceptible to being bred by disreputable, high profit puppy mills or "commercial breeders".

The puppy mill, inhumane and cruel world of canine pregnancy for profit occurs all over the world, and if you aren't very careful about where and how you purchase your Morkie puppy, you may unknowingly end up promoting this disreputable practice.

Not only do puppy mills seriously contribute to overpopulation, they produce diseases, and genetically flawed puppies that may suffer greatly with behavioral and/or health related problems that will cost their guardians greatly in terms of grief and stress and unexpected financial burden.

These dogs suffer in ways most of us could never imagine. For instance, most of these poor breeding dogs have never walked on solid ground or felt grass, as they are housed in cramped wire cages their entire short lives.

Females are bred continuously until they can no longer produce puppies, at which time they are sold to laboratories for experiments, killed or dumped on the side of a road.

Although the puppy mill problem is certainly not exclusive to the United States, as it happens all over the world, the problem is so rampant in the United States that several states are actually labelled as puppy mill states. These include Missouri, Nebraska, Kansas, Iowa, Arkansas, Oklahoma and Pennsylvania.

It can be difficult to shut down these mill operations because, just like the drug trade, it is business on a large and lucrative scale. As an example, in Missouri alone, it is estimated that the commercial puppy breeding industry nets $40 million dollars (£24,068,800) a year.

Although puppy mill puppies are sold in a variety of different venues, pet stores are the main source for selling these unfortunate puppies, who are taken away from their mothers far too young (at 4 to 5 weeks of age) and sold to brokers, who pack them into crates to ship them off to pet stores. Many innocent puppies die during transportation.

Think seriously before buying a puppy from a pet store, because almost all puppies found in pet stores are the result of inhumane puppy mill breeding, and if you purchase one of these puppies, you are helping to enable and perpetuate this horribly cruel breeding practice.

Every time someone buys a puppy from a pet store, the store will order more from the puppy mill. As far as the pet store is concerned, the puppies are simply inventory, like bags of dog food, and when one item drops off of the inventory list, another is purchased to replace it.

Puppy mill puppies are also sold at flea markets, on the side of the road, at the beach, through newspaper ads and through fancy websites and Internet classifieds.

The only way to put these shameful, commercial businesses out of business is by spreading the word and never buying a puppy from a pet store, or any other advertising medium, unless you have first thoroughly checked them out by visiting the facility in person.

Always be wary if you answer an advertisement for a puppy for sale and the person selling offers to deliver the puppy to you, because this could easily be the first sign that you are about to be involved in an illegal puppy mill operation.

Educate yourself and spread the word to others about puppy mills, because this is the first step toward ensuring that yourself and everyone you know are never unknowingly involved in the suffering that is forced upon the breeding dogs and puppies trapped in a puppy mill operation.

Chapter 4: Choosing the Right Dog

1. Pros & Cons BEFORE You Buy

No matter what breed you may be considering as a possible candidate for sharing your home and life, this decision should never be entered into lightly.

As with any breed, those who may be considering a Morkie need to carry out research and make sure they have all the facts straight before taking the plunge, because there are always many important factors to keep in mind.

When considering a Morkie, which is a combination of two purebred canines (Yorkshire Terrier and Maltese), you will want to take into consideration the traits, temperaments, characteristics and health of both breeds, as it is entirely possible that the Morkie may inherit any number of both positive and negative qualities found in either the Maltese or the Yorkshire Terrier.

a) Pros of Morkie Ownership

The Morkie is considered to be a non-shedding dog, which means that this breed could be a good choice for allergy sufferers.

The Morkie is relatively long-lived, meaning that your Morkie will be your faithful companion for many years.

The small size of the Morkie makes them easy to transport and more suitable for those living in an apartment without access to a yard.

Most Morkies are playful and cuddly companions.

The smaller size of the Morkie means that they will have a smaller appetite, and therefore, a smaller budget will be required for treats and food.

The Morkie is usually very lovable and dedicated to their family, and with their keen sense of hearing, they will always alert you to anyone approaching.

The Morkie can be easily trained by a calm, caring guardian.

The Morkie can be a good choice for a family with older children looking for a small, playful and cuddly family dog.

b) Cons of Morkie Ownership

The Morkie is a long lived small dog, which means that choosing to be a guardian for this toy breed also means being prepared for a long term responsibility that could be in the order of a 12 to 15 year commitment.

The Morkie is a "toy" breed, which means that this would usually not be a good choice for families with young children who could inadvertently injure such a small dog.

The Morkie's small size also makes them susceptible to accidentally being injured simply by being stepped on, or sat on, or rolled on (if you allow them to sleep with you).

A small Morkie can be carried off by a large bird of prey, such as a hawk, eagle or owl.

As the Morkie is a feisty and energetic little dog, they can easily wiggle out of your arms when they want to get to something and if they jump or fall from several feet, they can break their legs.

The Morkie is a non-shedding breed, which means that if you are not able to groom your dog yourself, you will need to commit to regular trips to the professional groomers every six to eight weeks.

The Morkie soft coat needs to be brushed or combed on a daily basis in order to avoid tangles and matting, especially if the coat is allowed to grow long. Less daily coat maintenance will be required if the coat is kept short.

The Morkie, being a combination of two purebred canines known for having barking tendencies, may not be a good choice if you are worried about neighbors complaining about possible barking.

A Morkie can be feisty, spirited and energetic, requiring lots of activity to keep them happy.

The Morkie can have a demanding personality.

Some Morkies can become easily over-excited when greeting new people and situations.

The Morkie's smaller size can mean complications during spaying.

Finally, there is an argument that perhaps has some serious merit when considering purchasing a designer breed, such as the hybrid Morkie. Some believe that *"no decent dog breeder would cross breed their dogs. So that leaves creating designer dogs to unscrupulous breeders, backyard breeders and puppy mills."*

2. How to Choose the Right Puppy

Choosing the right puppy for your family and your lifestyle is more important than you might imagine.

Many people do not give serious enough thought to sharing their home with a new puppy before they actually bring one home.

For instance, many of us choose a puppy solely based on what it looks like, because the breed may currently be popular, or because their family had the same kind of dog when they were a child.

a) Important Questions

In order to be fair to ourselves, our family and the puppy we choose to share our lives with, we humans need to take a serious look at our life, both as it is today and what we envision it being in the next ten to fifteen years and then ask ourselves a few important, personal questions, before making the commitment to a puppy, including:

(1) Do I have the time and patience necessary to devote to a puppy that will grow into a dog who needs a great deal of attention, training and endless amounts of my devotion?

(2) Do I lead a physically active, medium or low intensity life? For instance, am I out jogging the streets daily or climbing mountains or would I rather spend my leisure time on the couch?

(3) Do I like to travel a lot? Perhaps a dog small enough to travel in the plane cabin with me is a consideration.

(4) Am I a neat freak? A non-shedding breed such as the Morkie, would make more sense.

(5) Do I have a young, growing family that takes up all my spare time? A dog needs a lot of time and attention.

(6) Am I physically fit and healthy enough to be out there walking a dog two to three times a day, every day, rain or shine (and much more when it's just a puppy)?

(7) Can I afford the food costs and the veterinarian expenses that are part of being a conscientious dog guardian?

(8) Is the decision to bring a puppy into my life a family decision, or just for the children, who will quickly lose interest?

(9) What is the number one reason why I want a dog in my life?

Once you ask yourself these important questions and honestly answer them, you will have a much better understanding of the type of puppy that would be best suited for you and your family, and whether or not, it should be a Morkie.

If you choose the wrong dog, you will inevitably end up with an unhappy dog, which will lead to behavioral issues. Please take the time to choose wisely.

If you have absolutely decided the Morkie is the right dog for you, the following will help you to choose the right puppy from the litter.

b) Careful Puppy Selection

Although your breeder can often help you with selecting the right puppy for you and your family, you will probably be feeling especially drawn to one puppy over another.

Although there are other considerations, how you feel toward a particular puppy in a litter is also an important part of deciding which pup to bring home.

Beyond your feelings, considering other factors will help improve the odds of you having a positive guardianship experience with your new Morkie puppy.

For instance, being a little objective when evaluating each puppy in the litter will help you to make the right choice.

While some people become very emotional when choosing a puppy and will be attracted to those who display extremes in behavior because they want to *"save"* them, it is not particularly good advice to choose a puppy that may be very shy or frightened in the hope that they may grow into a happy, well-behaved dog.

Some people will delve even further into their emotional desires or needs to *"save"* or *"rescue"* and will choose a particular puppy because it has obvious health or behavioral issues and they want to provide it with a chance that they believe the puppy might not otherwise have.

While it is certainly wonderful that we humans have the capacity to raise and care for puppies that may be afflicted with health or behavior problems, it's important that these types of decisions are not undertaken lightly as such challenges can be a daunting undertaking.

While many minor behavioral problems can be modified with early training, it's important to be aware that the time and effort needed to do so will be difficult to predict.

c) Puppy Check List

Generally speaking, when choosing a puppy out of a litter, look for one that is friendly and outgoing, rather than one who is overly aggressive or fearful.

Taking note of a puppy's social skills, when they are still with their litter mates, will help you to choose the right puppy to take home, because puppies who demonstrate good social skills with their litter mates are much more likely to develop into easy going, happy adults who play well with other dogs.

In a social setting where all the puppies can be observed together, take notice:

a) during play, which puppies are comfortable both on top and on the bottom when play fighting and wresting with their litter mates, and which puppies seem to only like being on top. Puppies who don't mind being on the bottom or who appear to be fine with either position, will usually play well other dogs when they become adults.

b) if the puppies have toys to play with, observe which puppies try to keep the toys away from the other puppies and which puppies share. Those who want the toys to themselves may be more aggressive with other dogs or in play where toys are involved as they become older.

c) which puppies seem to like the company of the other pups and which ones seem to be loners. Puppies who like the company of their litter mates are more likely to be interested in the company of other dogs as they mature than puppies who are anti-social.

d) the reaction of puppies who get yelped at when they bite or roughhouse with another puppy too hard. Puppies who ease up when another puppy yelps or cries are more likely to respond appropriately when they play too roughly as adults.

Also, check to see if the puppy you are interested in is sociable with people, because if they will not come to you, or display fear to strangers, this may be a problem when they become adults.

Further, always check if the puppy you are interested in is relaxed about being handled, because if they are not, they may become difficult with adults and children during daily interactions, during grooming or visits to the veterinarian's office.

3. How to Check If a Puppy is Healthy

Of course you will want to check if a puppy you are considering taking home is not just emotionally healthy, but also physically healthy.

First, ask to see veterinarian reports from the breeder to satisfy yourself that the puppy is as healthy as possible, and then once you make your decision to share your life with a particular puppy, make an appointment with your own veterinarian for a complete examination.

Before you get to this stage, however, there are a few general signs of good health to be aware of when choosing a healthy puppy from a litter, including the following:

- **Breathing**: they will breathe quietly, without coughing or sneezing, and there will be no crusting or discharge around their nostrils;

- **Body**: they will look round and well fed, with an obvious layer of fat over their rib cage;

- **Coat**: they will have a soft, shiny coat with no dandruff, dullness, greasiness or bald spots;

- **Energy**: a well rested puppy should be alert and energetic;

- **Hearing**: a puppy should react if you clap your hands behind their head;

- **Genitals**: they will not have any sort of discharge visible in or around their genital or anal region;

- **Mobility**: they will walk and run normally without wobbling, limping or seeming to be stiff or sore; and

- **Vision**: they will have bright, clear eyes without crust or discharge and they should notice a ball rolling past within their field of vision.

4. One Morkie, or Two?

While getting two Morkie puppies at once will be double the fun, it will also be double the work, which means as their human guardian, you will need to be doubly alert and patient, and perhaps also lose even more sleep than you bargained for during the potty training phase.

Every puppy needs your constant attention and guidance, therefore, before taking the plunge, ask yourself if you have the time and energy to provide constant attention and guidance for two little puppies?

Many humans decide to get two puppies because they want their puppy to have someone to play with, and one of the reasons for this decision might be based on the fact that the human making this decision might not be the ideal candidate for having one puppy, let alone two.

For instance, if the reason you are considering two puppies is so that the one puppy will not be alone all day while you are at work, stop right there, because leaving one, two or a dozen puppies alone all day while you are at work is a terrible decision and you should NOT be considering any puppy at this stage of your life.

Another consideration when thinking about whether or not to get two puppies, is that often when they grow up, there may be continual sibling rivalry, as each puppy vies for your attention.

What often happens when the puppies mature is that they stop getting along with each other, and their relationship may deteriorate to the point where they no longer enjoy each other's company.

Further, when you have two puppies growing up together, one will always be the more dominant personality that will take over the other, and this could mean that neither puppy will fully develop their individual personalities.

As well, when you have two puppies or dogs in your life, they generally tend to be less affectionate or interested in their human guardians, as they have each other in their own pack of dogs to rely upon. This can mean that they will focus so much on each other that they will bond much less with you, which can make it more difficult to train or convince either that you are the actual leader of the pack.

Each puppy will require your individual attention when it comes time for training, and having two puppies in the picture can make it very difficult for them to concentrate or focus on the job at hand.

For instance, when you are teaching puppy #1 to "Sit" and puppy #2 is trying to bite their tail, your job is going to be much more challenging. The only way to properly accomplish training sessions with two puppies will be to lock one of the puppies in another room so that they each have their one on one time with you.

Bottom line, most professional trainers will advise that if you want two puppies, not to get them at the exact same time, from the same litter, so that you have the opportunity to house train and teach basic commands to one puppy before you bring another one into the home.

5. Best Age to Purchase a Morkie Puppy

Generally speaking, no puppy, including a Morkie puppy, should be removed from their mother any earlier than 8 weeks of age and leaving them until they are **10 to 16 weeks of age is preferred,** because this will give them the time to learn important life skills from the mother dog, including eating solid food and grooming.

Furthermore, leaving a puppy amongst their litter mates for a longer period of time will help to ensure that they learn socialization skills.

Removing a puppy from the mother and other siblings too early could mean that they will miss out on valuable skills, and may not socialize well with others.

For the first month of a puppy's life they will be on a mother's milk only diet. Once the puppy's teeth begin to appear, they will start to be weaned from mother's milk and by the age of 8 weeks should be completely weaned and eating just puppy food.

Removing a puppy from their mother any earlier than eight weeks could mean they are not fully weaned and they would be much more difficult to feed.

6. Should I Get a Male or Female?

Everyone you ask will have their own opinions about whether you should get a male or a female Morkie. While you will find just as many humans preferring a male Morkie over a female Morkie, there may be a few considerations that can help you to make a more informed decision.

Male dogs tend to want to mark or pee on anything upright (trees, telephone poles, tall grass, a stranger's leg) wherever they are out walking much more than females, however, a dominant female will also mark territory.

A male Morkie, even a housebroken one, may try to lift their leg on furniture when visiting the home where there are other dogs present.

When spaying and neutering your Morkie, the operation is much more invasive when spaying a small female than the neutering process required for males.

Some humans pick their dogs based on sex alone because they cannot stop themselves from attributing human characteristics to their chosen dogs, and therefore believe that, for instance, a female dog will have a "sweeter" temperament, or a male dog may be more "independent".

Of course, a dog is a dog, and it does no good to imagine that they will act like humans just because we are human.

Therefore, the best way to choose your Morkie puppy will be to take your time observing the litter when you visit the breeder.

7. The Morkie Shopping List

Before bringing home your new Morkie for the first time, there will be a list of items you need to make sure you have on hand, including:

- Food – usually, the puppy will remain on whatever food they have been fed at the breeder's for at least the first couple of weeks, until they are well settled in their new home, so make sure you ask the breeder what brand to buy;

- Food and Water Bowls - make sure they are small enough for a young Morkie puppy to get into so that they can easily eat and drink. I suggest a durable stainless dining set that can later be used as travel bowls;

- Kennel - when you buy your puppy's hard-sided kennel, make sure that you buy the size that will be appropriate for them when they are fully grown. It must be large enough so that (when fully grown) they can easily stand up and turn around inside it;

- Martingale collar, 2 Leashes and Harness - buy the harness and collar small enough to fit your puppy and buy new ones as they grow larger. You will be able to keep the same leashes, as all you will ever need is a four foot (1.22 meters) leash made out of nylon webbing, with a light weight clip at the end (do not buy a leash that has a heavy clip on the end, as it will be difficult for your tiny puppy to carry around);

- Soft beds (one or two) for them to sleep in when they are not in their kennel - get the beds large enough for a fully grown Morkie;

- *"Sherpa"* or another type of soft-sided travel bag to get them used to traveling inside a carrier bag - get the bag large enough to fit them when they are fully grown and take it with you when you pick up your puppy from the breeder;

- Shampoo and Conditioner;

- Finger tooth brush - this is a soft rubber cap that fits over the human's finger to get the puppy used to having their teeth regularly brushed;

- Soft bristle brush and comb - for daily grooming;

- Puppy nail scissors - for trimming their toenails;

- Small blunt nosed grooming scissors - for trimming the hair around their eyes;

- One or two soft toys, or wait until they come home and let them pick their own toys from the store;

- Puppy sized treats;

- Poop bags;

- Pee pads;

- Bath towels;

- Non-slip mat for the sink or tub.

Be sure to take your Morkie shopping list with you when you go to your local pet store or boutique, otherwise you may forget critical items.

8. Puppy Proofing Your Home

Most puppies will be a curious bundle of energy, which means that they will get into everything within their reach.

As a responsible puppy guardian, you will want to provide a safe environment for them, which means eliminating all sources of danger, similar to what you would do for a curious toddler.

Be aware that your Morkie puppy will want to touch, sniff, taste, investigate and closely inspect every electrical cord, every closet, every nook and cranny of your home and everything you may have left lying about on the floor.

Power cords can be found in just about every room in the home and to a teething puppy, these may look like irresistible, fun, chew toys. Make sure that you tuck all power cords securely out of your puppy's reach or enclose them inside a chew-proof PVC tube.

Kitchen: first of all, there are many human foods that can be harmful to dogs, therefore, your kitchen should always be strictly off limits to your puppy any time you are preparing food. Calmly send them out of the kitchen any time you are in the kitchen, and they will quickly get the idea that this area is off limits to them.

Bathroom: bathroom cupboards and drawers or the side of a bathtub where you may leave your shaving supplies can hold many dangers for a young and curious Morkie puppy.

Kleenex, cotton swabs, Q-tips, toilet paper, razors, pills, and soap left within your puppy's reach are an easy target that could result in an emergency visit to your veterinarian's office.

Family members need to put shampoos, soap, facial products, makeup and accessories out of reach or safely inside a cabinet or drawer.

Bedroom: if you don't keep your shoes, slippers and clothing safely behind doors, you may find that your puppy has claimed them for their new chew toys. Be vigilant about keeping everything in its safe place, including jewelry, hair ties, bills, coins, and other items small enough for them to swallow in containers or drawers, and secure any exposed cords or wires.

If you have children, make sure they understand that, especially while your puppy is going through their teething stage, that they must keep their rooms picked up and leave nothing that could cause a choking problem to the puppy laying about on the floor or within their reach.

Living Room: we humans often spend many hours in our cozy gathering places to watch movies or play games, and often, the living areas of our homes will have many items that are very enticing for a curious and teething puppy, such as books, magazines, pillows, iPods, TV remotes and more.

You will want to keep your home free of excess clutter and remain vigilant about straightening up and putting things out of sight that could be tempting to your puppy.

Office: we humans often spend a great deal of time in our home offices, which means that our puppy will want to be there, too, and they will be curious about all the items an office has to offer, including papers, books, magazines, and electrical cords.

Although your puppy might think that rubber bands or paper clips are fun to play with, allowing these items to be within your puppy's reach could end up being a fatal mistake if your puppy swallows them.

Plants: are also a very tempting target for your puppy's teeth, so you will want to keep them well out their reach. If you have floor plants, they will need to be moved to a shelf or counter or placed behind a closed door until your curious fur friend grows out of the habit of putting everything in their mouth. Also keep in mind that many common house plants are poisonous to dogs.

Garage and Yard: there are obvious as well as subtle dangers that could seriously harm, or even kill, a Morkie puppy that are often found in the garage or yard. Some of these might include antifreeze, gasoline, fertilizers, rat and mice poison, snail and slug poison, weed killer, paint, cleaners and solvents, grass seed, bark mulch and various insecticides.

If you are storing any of these toxic substances in your garage or garden shed, make certain that you keep all such bottles, boxes, or containers inside a locked cabinet, or stored on high shelves that your puppy will not be able to reach. Even better, choose not to use toxic chemicals anywhere in your home or yard.

9. Puppy Hazard Home Inspection

Every conscientious puppy guardian needs to take a serious look around the home not just from the human eye level, but from the eye level of a Morkie puppy. This means literally crawling around your floors.

Your puppy has a much lower vantage point than you do when standing, therefore, there may be items in your environment that could potentially be harmful to a Morkie puppy that a human might not notice unless you get down on the floor and take a really good look.

10. First Weeks With Your Puppy

a) The First Night

Before you go to the breeder's to pick up your new Morkie puppy, vacuum your floors and do a last minute check of every room to make sure that everything that could be a puppy hazard is carefully tucked away out of sight and that nothing is left on the floor or low down on shelves where a curious puppy might get into trouble.

Close most of the doors inside your home, so that there is just one or two rooms that the puppy will have access to.

You have already been shopping and have everything you need, so get out a puppy pee pad and have it at the ready when you bring your new fur friend home.

Also have your soft bed(s) in an area where you will be spending most of your time and where they will be easily found by your puppy. If you have already purchased a soft toy, leave it in your puppy's soft bed, or take the toy with you when you go to pick up your puppy.

NOTE: take either your hard-sided kennel or your soft-sided "Sherpa" travel bag with you when going to bring your new puppy home, and make sure that it is securely fastened to the seat of your vehicle with the seatbelt system and lined with a puppy pee pad.

Even though you will be tempted to hold your new Morkie puppy in your lap on the drive home, this is a very dangerous place for them to be, in case of an accident.

Place them inside their kennel or bag, which will be lined with soft towels and perhaps even a warm, towel wrapped hot water bottle, and close the door. If you have a friend who can drive for you, sit beside them in the back seat, and if they cry on the way home, remind them that they are not alone with your soft, soothing voice.

Before bringing your new Morkie puppy inside your home, take them to the place where you want them to relieve themselves and try to wait it out long enough for them to at least go pee.

Then bring them inside your home and introduce them to the area where their food and water bowls will be kept, in case they are hungry or thirsty.

Let them wander around sniffing and checking out their new surroundings and gently encourage them to follow you wherever you go.

Show them where the puppy pee pad is located and place it near the door where you will exit to take them outside to relieve themselves. Many pee pads are scented to encourage a puppy to pee, and if they do, happily praise them.

Show them where their hard-sided kennel is (in your bedroom) and put them inside with the door open while you sit on the floor in front and quietly encourage them to relax inside their kennel.

Depending on the time of day when you bring your new Morkie puppy home for the first time, practice this kennel exercise several times throughout the day, and if they will take a little treat each time you encourage them to go inside their kennel, this will help to further encourage the behavior of wanting to go inside.

After they have had their evening meal, take them outside approximately 20 minutes later to relieve themselves, and when they do, make sure you are very enthusiastic with your praise and perhaps even give a little treat.

So far your Morkie puppy has only been allowed in several rooms of your home, as you have kept the other doors closed, so keep it this way for the first few days.

Before it's time for bed, again take your puppy outside for a very short walk to the same place where they last relieved themselves and make sure that they go pee before bringing them back inside.

Before bed, prepare your Morkie puppy's hot water bottle and wrap it in a towel so that it will not be too hot for them, and place it inside their hard-sided kennel (in your bedroom).

Turn the lights down low and invite your puppy to go inside their kennel and if they seem interested, perhaps give them a soft toy to have inside with them. Let them walk into the kennel under their own steam and when they do, give them a little treat (if they are interested) and encourage them to snuggle down to sleep while you are sitting on the floor in front of the kennel.

Once they have settled down inside their kennel, close the door, go to your bed and turn all the lights off. It may help your puppy to sleep during their first night home, if you can play quiet, soothing music in the background.

If they start to cry or whine, stay calm and have compassion because this is the first time in their young life when they do not have the comfort of their mother or their litter mates. Do not let them out of their kennel, simply reassure them with your calm voice that they are not alone until they fall asleep.

b) The First Week

During the first week, you and your new Morkie puppy will be getting settled into their new routine, which will involve you getting used to your puppy's needs as they also get used to your usual schedule.

Be as consistent as possible with your waking and sleeping routine, getting up and going to bed at the same time each day, so that it will be easier for your puppy to get into the flow of their new life.

First thing in the morning, remove your puppy from their kennel and take them immediately outside to relieve themselves at the place where they last went pee.

At this time, if you are teaching them to ring a doorbell to go outside, let them ring the bell before you go out the door with them, whether you are carrying them, or whether they are walking out the door on their own.

NOTE: during the first week, you may want to carry your puppy outside first thing in the morning as they may not be able to hold it for very long once waking up.

When you bring them back inside, you can let them follow you so they get used to their new leash and/or harness arrangement.

Be very careful not to drag your puppy if they stop or pull back on the leash. If they refuse to walk on the leash, just hold the tension toward you (without pulling) while encouraging them to walk toward you, until they start to move forward again.

Now it will be time for their first feed of the day, and after they have finished eating, keep an eye on the clock, because you will want to take them outside to relieve themselves in about 20 minutes.

When your puppy is not eating or napping, they will be wanting to explore and have little play sessions with you and these times will help you bond with your puppy more and more each day.

As their new guardian, it will be your responsibility to keep a close eye on them throughout the day, so that you can notice when they need to relieve themselves and either take them to their pee pad or take them outside.

You will also need to make sure that they are eating and drinking enough throughout the day, so set regular feeding times at least three times a day.

Also set specific times in the day when you will take your puppy out for a little walk on leash and harness, so that they are not only going outside when they need to relieve themselves, but they are also learning to explore their new neighborhood with you beside them.

When your Morkie puppy is still very young, you will not want to walk for a long time, as they will get tired easily, so keep your walks to no more than 15 or 20 minutes during your first week and if they seem tired or cold, pick them up and carry them home.

11. Common Mistakes to Avoid

a) Sleeping in Your Bed

Many of us make the mistake of allowing a crying puppy to sleep with us in our bed, and while this may help to calm and comfort a new puppy, it will set a dangerous precedent that can result in behavioral problems later in their life.

Also, a tiny Morkie puppy can easily be crushed by a sleeping human body.

As much as it may pull on your heart strings to hear your new Morkie puppy crying the first couple of nights in their kennel, a little tough love at the beginning will help them to learn to both love and respect you as their leader.

b) Picking Them Up at the Wrong Time

Never pick your puppy up if they display fear or growl at an object or person, because this will be rewarding them for unbalanced behavior.

Instead, your puppy needs to be gently corrected by you, with firm and calm energy so that they learn not to react with fear or aggression.

c) Playing Too Hard or Too Long

Many humans play too hard or allow their children to play too long with a young puppy. You need to remember that a young puppy tires very easily and especially during the critical growing phases of their young life, they need their rest.

d) Hand Play

Always discourage your Morkie puppy from chewing or biting your hands, or any part of your body for that matter. If you allow them to do this when they are puppies, they will want to continue to do so when they have strong jaws and adult teeth and this is not acceptable behavior for any breed of dog.

Do not get into the habit of playing the *"hand"* game, where you rough up the puppy and slide them across the floor with your hands, because this will teach your puppy that your hands are play things.

When your puppy is teething, they will naturally want to chew on everything within reach, and this will include you. As cute as you might think it is, this is not an acceptable behavior and you need to gently, but firmly, discourage the habit.

A light flick with a finger on the end of the nose, combined with a firm "NO" when they are trying to bite human fingers will discourage them from this activity.

e) Distraction and Replacement

When your puppy tries to chew on your hand, foot, or your clothing, or anything else that is not fair game, you need to firmly and calmly tell them "No", and then distract them by replacing what they are not supposed to be chewing with their chew toy.

Make sure that you happily praise them every time they choose the toy to chew on.

If the puppy persists in chewing on you, remove yourself from the equation by getting up and walking away. If they are really persistent, put them inside their kennel with a favorite chew toy until they calm down.

Always praise your puppy when they stop inappropriate behavior so that they begin to understand what they can and cannot do.

12. Bonding With Your Morkie

You will begin bonding with your Morkie puppy from the very first moment you bring them home from the breeders.

This is the time when your puppy will be the most distraught, as they will no longer have the guidance, warmth and comfort of their mother or their other litter mates, and you will need to take on the role of being your new puppy's center of attention.

Be patient and kind with them as they are learning you are now their new center of the universe.

Your daily interaction with your puppy during play sessions, and especially your disciplined exercises, including going for walks on leash, and teaching commands and tricks, will be the best bonding opportunities.

Do not make the mistake of thinking that *"bonding"* with your new puppy can only happen if you are playing or cuddling together, because the very best bonding happens when you are kindly teaching rules and boundaries.

Chapter 5: House Training

1. Human Training

House training, or "potty" training, is a critical first step in the education of any new puppy, and the first part of of a successful process is training the human guardian.

When you bring home your new Morkie puppy, they will be relying upon your guidance to teach them what they need to learn.

When you provide your puppy with your consistent patience and understanding, they are capable of learning rules at a very early age, and house training is no different, especially since it's all about establishing a regular routine.

Potty training a new puppy takes time and patience — how much time depends entirely upon you.

Check in with yourself and make sure your energy remains consistently calm and patient and that you exercise plenty of compassion and understanding while you help your new puppy learn the new bathroom rules.

Morkie puppies and dogs flourish with routines and happily, so do humans, therefore, the first step is to establish a daily routine that will work well for both canine and human alike.

For instance, depending upon the age of your Morkie puppy, make a plan to take them out for a bathroom break every two hours and stick to it because while you are in the beginning stages of potty training, the more vigilant and consistent you can be, the quicker and more successful your results will be.

Generally speaking, while your puppy is still growing, a young puppy can hold it approximately one hour for every month of their age.

This means that if your 2-month-old puppy has been happily snoozing for a couple of hours, as soon as they wake up, they will need to go outside.

Some of the first indications or signs that your puppy needs to be taken outside to relieve themselves will be when you see them:

- sniffing around
- circling
- looking for the door
- whining, crying or barking
- acting agitated

It will be important to always take your Morkie puppy out first thing every morning, and immediately after they wake up from a nap as well as soon after they have finished eating a meal or having a big drink of water.

Also, your happy praise goes a long way toward encouraging and reinforcing future success when your Morkie puppy makes the right decisions, so let them know you are happy when they do their business in the right place.

Initially, treats can be a good way to reinforce how happy you are that your puppy is learning to relieve themselves in the right place. Slowly treats can be removed and replaced with your happy praise.

Next, now that you have a new puppy in your life, you will want to be flexible with respect to adapting your schedule to meet the requirements that will help to quickly teach your Morkie puppy their new bathroom routine.

This means not leaving your puppy alone for endless hours at a time because firstly, they are pack animals that need companionship and your direction at all times, plus long periods alone will result in the disruption of the potty training schedule you have worked hard to establish.

If you have no choice but to leave your puppy alone for many hours, make sure that you place them in a paper lined room or pen where they can relieve themselves without destroying your favorite carpet.

Remember, your Morkie is a growing puppy with a bladder and bowels that they do not yet have complete control over and you will have a much happier time and better success if you simply train yourself to pay attention to when your young companion is showing signs of needing to relieve themselves.

2. Bell Training

A very easy way to introduce your new Morkie puppy to house training is to begin by teaching them how to ring a doorbell whenever they need to go outside.

Ringing a doorbell is not only a convenient alert system for both you and your Morkie puppy or dog, your visitors will be most impressed by how smart your Morkie is.

A further benefit of training your puppy to ring a bell is that you will not have to listen to your puppy or dog whining, barking or howling to be let out, and your door will not become scratched up from their nails.

Unless you prefer to purchase an already manufactured doggy doorbell or system, take a trip to your local novelty store and purchase a small bell that has a nice, loud ring.

Attach the bell to a piece of ribbon or string and hang it from a door handle or tape it to a door sill near the door where you will be taking your puppy out when they need to relieve themselves. The string will need to be long enough so that your Morkie puppy can easily reach the bell with their nose or a paw.

Next, each time you take your puppy out to relieve themselves, say the word *"Out"*, and use their paw or their nose to ring the bell. Praise them for this "trick" and immediately take them outside.

The only down side to teaching your Morkie puppy or dog to ring a bell when they want to go outside, is that even if they don't actually have to go out to relieve themselves, but just want to go outside because they are bored, you will still have to take them out every time they ring the bell.

There are many types and styles of *"gotta' go"* commercially manufactured bells you could choose, ranging from the elegant **"Poochie Bells™"** that hang from a doorknob, the simple **"Tell Bell™"** that sits on the floor, or various high tech door chime systems that function much like a doggy intercom system where they push a pad with their paw and it rings a bell.

Whatever doorbell system you choose for your Morkie puppy, once they are trained, this type of an alert system is an easy way to eliminate accidents in the home.

3. Kennel Training

Kennel training is always a good idea for any puppy early in their education, because it can be utilized for many different situations, including being a very helpful tool for house training.

When purchasing a kennel for your Morkie puppy, always buy a kennel that will be the correct size for your Morkie puppy once they become adult size. The kennel will be the correct size if your full grown Morkie dog can stand up and easily turn around inside their kennel.

When you train your Morkie puppy to accept sleeping in their own kennel at nighttime, this will also help to accelerate their potty training, because no puppy or dog wants to relieve themselves where they sleep, which means that they will hold their bladder and bowels as long as they possibly can.

Always be kind and compassionate and remember that a puppy will be able to hold it approximately one hour for every month of their age.

Generally, a Morkie puppy who is three months old, will be able to hold it for approximately three hours, unless they just ate a meal or had a big drink of water.

Be watchful and consistent so that you learn your Morkie puppy's body language, and when it's time for them to go outside. Presenting them with familiar scents, by taking them to the same spot in the yard or the same street corner, will help to remind and encourage them that they are outside to relieve themselves.

Use a voice cue to remind your puppy why they are outside, such as *"go pee"* and always remember to praise them every time they relieve themselves in the right place so that they quickly understand what you expect of them and will learn to "go" on cue.

4. Exercise Pen Training

The exercise pen is a transition from kennel only training and will be helpful for those times when you may have to leave your Morkie puppy for more hours than they can reasonably be expected to hold it.

During those times when you must be away from the home for several hours, it's time to introduce your Morkie puppy to an exercise pen.

Exercise pens are usually constructed of wire sections that you can put together in whatever shape you desire, and the pen needs to be large enough to hold your puppy's kennel on one half of the pen, while the other half will be lined with newspapers or pee pads.

Place your Morkie puppy's food and water dishes next to the kennel and leave the kennel door open, so they can wander in and out whenever they wish, to eat or drink or go to the papers if they need to relieve themselves.

Your puppy will be contained in a small area of your home while you are away and because they are already used to sleeping inside their kennel, they will not want to relieve themselves inside the area where they sleep. Therefore, your Morkie puppy will naturally go to the other half of the pen to relieve themselves on the newspapers or pee pads.

This method will help train your puppy to be quickly paper trained when you have to be away for a few hours.

5. Puppy Apartment™ Training

While a similar concept and a more costly alternative, the *Puppy Apartment*™ is a step up from the exercise pen training system that makes the process of crate or pen training even easier on both humans and puppies.

The Puppy Apartment™ works well in a variety of situations, whether you're at home and unable to pay close attention to your Morkie puppy's needs, whether you must be away from the home for a few hours or during the evening when everyone is asleep, and you don't particularly want to get up at 3:00 a.m. to take your Morkie puppy out to go pee. The Puppy Apartment™ is an innovation that is convenient for both puppy and human alike.

What makes this system so effective is the patent pending dividing wall with a door leading to the other side, all inside the pen. One side of the Puppy Apartment™ is where the puppy's bed is located and the other side (through the doorway), is the bathroom area that is lined with pee pads.

With the bathroom right next door, your Morkie puppy or dog can relieve themselves whenever they wish, without the need to alert family members to let them out.

This one bedroom, one bathroom system, which is a combination of the kennel/training pen, is a great alternative for helping to eliminate the stress of worrying about always keeping a watchful eye on your puppy or getting up in the night to take them outside every few hours to help them avoid making mistakes.

According to *"Modern Puppies"*...

> *"The Puppy Apartment™ takes the MESSY out of paper training, the ODORS AND HASSLES out of artificial grass training, MISSING THE MARK out of potty pad training and HAVING TO HOLD IT out of crate training. House training a puppy has never been faster or easier!*
>
> *The Puppy Apartment™ has taken all the benefits of the most popular potty training methods and combined them into one magical device and potty training system. This*

device and system has revolutionized how modern puppies are potty trained!"

Manufactured in the United States, this product ships directly from the California supplier (Modern Puppies).

The price of the Puppy Apartment™ begins at $138. USD (£83.37) and is only available online at Modern Puppies.

6. Free Training

If you would rather not confine your young Morkie puppy to one or two rooms in your home, and will be allowing them to freely range about your home anywhere they wish during the day, this is considered free training.

When free house training your Morkie puppy, you will need to closely watch your puppy's activities all day long so that you can be aware of the *"signs"* that will indicate when they need to go outside to relieve themselves.

For instance, circling and sniffing is a sure sign that they are looking for a place to do their business.

Never get upset or scold a puppy for having an accident inside the home, because this will result in teaching your puppy to be afraid of you and to only relieve themselves in secret places or when you're not watching.

If you catch your Morkie puppy making a mistake, all that is necessary is for you to calmly say *"No"*, and quickly scoop them up and take them outside or to their indoor bathroom area. From your puppy's point of view, yelling or screaming when they make a potty mistake, is unstable energy being displayed by the person who is supposed to be their leader and this type of behavior will only teach your puppy to fear and disrespect you.

The Morkie is not a difficult puppy to housebreak and they will generally do very well when you start them off with *"puppy pee pads"* that you will move closer and closer to the same door that you always use when taking them outside. This way they will quickly learn to associate going to this door when they need to relieve themselves.

When you pay close attention to your Morkie puppy's sleeping, eating, drinking and playing habits, you will quickly learn their body language so that you are able to predict when they might need to relieve themselves.

Your Morkie puppy will always need to relieve themselves first thing in the morning, as soon as they wake up from a nap, approximately 20 minutes after they finish eating a meal, after they have finished a play session, and of course, before they go to bed at night.

It's important to have compassion during this house training time in your young Morkie's life so that their education will be as stress-free as possible.

It's also important to be vigilant because how well you pay attention will minimize the opportunities your puppy may have for making a bathroom mistake in the first place, and the fewer mistakes they make, the sooner your Morkie puppy will be house trained.

7. Professional Cleaning Products

Remember that a dog's sense of smell is at least 2,000 times more sensitive that our human sense of smell.

As a result of your Morkie puppy's superior sense of smell, it will be very important to effectively remove all odors from house training accidents, because otherwise, your Morkie puppy will be attracted by the smell to the place where they may have had a previous accident, and will want to do their business there again and again.

While there are many products that are supposed to remove odors and stains, many of these are not very effective. You want a professional grade cleaner that will not just mask one odor with another scent, you want a product that will completely neutralize odors.

TIP: go to RemoveUrineOdors.com and order yourself some *"SUN"* and/or *"Max Enzyme"* because these products contain professional-strength odor neutralizers and urine digesters that bind to and completely absorb odors on any type of surface.

Chapter 6: Medical Care & Safety

1. Choosing a Veterinarian

A consideration to keep in mind when choosing a veterinarian clinic will be that some clinics specialize in caring for smaller pets, and some specialize in larger animal care, while others have a wide ranging area of expertise and will care for all animals, including reptiles.

Choosing a clinic will be a personal decision, however, since the Morkie is considered a small or "toy" breed of dog, your dog's needs may be better served by choosing a clinic that specializes in smaller pets.

Choosing a good veterinary clinic will be very similar to choosing the right health care clinic or doctor for your own personal health because you want to ensure that your Morkie puppy receives the quality care they deserve.

Start your search by asking other dog owners where they take their dogs and whether they are happy with the service they receive.

If you don't know anyone to ask, visit the local pet store in your area who will be able to provide you with references and local listings of pet care clinics.

Next, check online, because a good pet clinic will have an active website up and running that will list details of all the services they provide along with an overview of all staff members, their education and qualifications.

Once you've narrowed your search, it's time to personally visit the clinics you may be interested in, as this will be a good opportunity for you to visually inspect the facility, interact with the staff and meet the veterinarians face to face.

Of course, it's not just you who needs to feel comfortable with the clinic chosen and those working there. Your puppy needs to feel comfortable, too, and this is where visiting a clinic and interacting with the staff and veterinarians will show you their experience and expertise in handling your puppy.

If your puppy is comfortable with them, then you will be much more likely to trust that they will be providing the best care for your puppy who will need to receive all their puppy vaccinations and eventually be spayed or neutered.

It's also a good idea to take your puppy into your chosen clinic several times before they actually need to be there, so that they are not fearful of the new smells and unfamiliar surroundings.

2. Neutering and Spaying

While it can sometimes be difficult to find the definitive answer about when the best time to neuter or spay your young Morkie is, because there are varying opinions on this topic, one thing that most veterinarians do agree on is that earlier spaying or neutering, between 4 and 6 months of age, is a better choice than waiting.

Spaying or neutering surgeries are carried out under general anesthesia.

More dogs are being neutered at younger ages, so speak with your veterinarian and ask for their recommendations regarding the right age to spay or neuter your Morkie.

a) Effects on Aggression

Intact (non-neutered) males and females are more likely to display aggression related to sexual behavior than neutered animals. Fighting, particularly in males, that is directed at other males, is less common after neutering.

The intensity of other types of aggression, such as irritable aggression in females will be totally eliminated by spaying.

While neutering or spaying is not a treatment for aggression, it can certainly help to minimize the severity and escalation of aggressiveness and is often the first step toward resolving an aggressive behavior problem.

b) What is Neutering?

Neutering is a surgical procedure, carried out by a licensed veterinarian surgeon, that renders a male dog unable to reproduce.

In males, the surgery is also referred to as *"castration"* because the procedure entails the removal of the young dog's testicles. When the testicles are removed, what is left behind is an empty scrotal sac (which used to contain the puppy's testicles) and this empty sac will soon shrink in size until it is no longer noticeable.

c) Neutering Males

Neutering male Morkie puppies before they are six months of age can help to ensure that they will be less likely to suffer from obesity as they grow older.

Neutering can also mean that a male Morkie will be less likely to have the urge to wander.

Further, waiting until a male Morkie is older than six months before having them neutered could mean that they will experience the effects of raging testosterone that will drive them to escape their yards by any means necessary to search out females to mate with.

Non-neutered males also tend to spray or mark territory far more, both inside and outside the home, and during this time can start to display aggressive tendencies toward other dogs as well as people.

d) What is Spaying?

In female puppies, sterilization, referred, to as *"spaying"*, is a surgical procedure carried out by a licensed veterinarian, to prevent the female dog from becoming pregnant and to stop regular heat cycles.

The sterilization procedure is much more involved for a female puppy (than for a male), as it requires the removal of both ovaries and the uterus by incision into the puppy's abdominal cavity. The uterus is also removed during this surgery, to prevent the possibility of it becoming infected later on in life.

e) Spaying Females

Preferably, female Morkie puppies should be spayed before their very first estrus or heat cycle. Females in heat often appear more agitated and irritable, while sleeping and eating less and some may become extremely aggressive toward other dogs.

Spaying female puppies before their first heat pattern can eliminate these hormonal stressors and reduce the opportunity of mammary glandular tumors. Early spaying also protects against various other potential concerns, such as uterine infections.

f) Effects on General Temperament

Many dog owners often become needlessly worried that a neutered or spayed dog will lose their vigor. Rest assured that a dog's personality or energy level will not be modified by neutering, and in fact, many unfavorable qualities resulting from hormonal impact may resolve after surgery.

Your Morkie will certainly not come to be less caring or cheerful, and neither will it resent you, because you are not denying your dog any essential encounters. You will, however, be acting as an accountable, informed, and caring Morkie owner.

Further, there is little evidence to suggest that the nature of a female Morkie will improve after having a litter of puppies.

It is important that you do not place your own psychological needs or concerns onto your Morkie puppy, because there is no gain to be had from permitting sexual activity in either male or female canines.

It is not "*abnormal*" or "*mean*" to manage a puppy's reproductive activity by having them sterilized. Rather, it is unkind not to neuter or spay a dog, as there are many benefits of having this procedure carried out.

g) Effects on Escape and Roaming

A neutered or spayed Morkie is less likely to wander. Castrated male dogs have the tendency to patrol smaller sized outdoor areas and are less likely to participate in territorial conflicts with perceived opponents.

NOTE: a Morkie that has actually already had successful escapes from the yard may continue to wander after they are spayed or neutered.

h) Effects on Problem Elimination

An unsterilized dog may urinate or defecate inside the home or in other undesirable areas in an attempt to stake territorial claims, relieve anxiety, or advertise their available reproductive status.

While neutering or spaying a Morkie puppy will reduce the more powerful urine odor as well as eliminate the hormonal factors, once this habit has begun, the undesirable behavior may continue to persist after neutering or spaying.

i) Possible Weight Gain

While metabolic changes that occur after spaying or neutering can cause some Morkie puppy's to gain weight, often the real culprit for any weight gain is the human who feels guilty for subjecting their puppy to any kind of pain and therefore, they attempt to make themselves feel better by feeding more treats or meals to their Morkie companion.

If you are concerned about weight gain after neutering or spaying a Morkie puppy, simply adjust their food and treat consumption, as needed.

It is a very simply process to change your Morkie's food intake according to their physical demands and how they look, and if your Morkie puppy's daily exercise and level of activity has not changed after they have been spayed or neutered, there will likely be no change in food management necessary.

3. Vaccinations

a) Why Vaccinate a Puppy?

Puppies are vaccinated by a veterinarian to provide them with protection against four common and serious diseases. Vaccination against these common sets of diseases is referred to as "*DAPP*", which stands for **D**istemper, **A**denovirus, **P**arainfluenza and **P**arvo Virus.

Approximately one week after your Morkie puppy has completed all three sets of primary vaccinations, they will be fully protected from those specific diseases. Then, most veterinarians will recommend a once a year vaccination for the next year or two.

It has now become common practice to vaccinate adult dogs every three years, and if your veterinarian is insisting on a yearly vaccination for your Morkie puppy, you need to ask them why, because to do otherwise is considered by most professionals to be *"over vaccinating"*.

b) Distemper

Canine distemper is a contagious and serious viral illness for which there is currently no known cure.

This deadly virus, which is spread either through the air or by direct or indirect contact with a dog that is already infected, or other distemper carrying wildlife, including ferrets, raccoons, foxes, skunks and wolves, is a relative of the measles virus which affects humans.

Canine distemper is sometimes also called "hard pad disease" because some strains of the distemper virus actually cause thickening of the pads on a dog's feet, which can also affect the end of a dog's nose.

In dogs or animals with weak immune systems, death may result two to five weeks after the initial infection.

Early symptoms of distemper include fever, loss of appetite, and mild eye inflammation that may only last a day or two. Symptoms become more serious and noticeable as the disease progresses.

A puppy or dog that survives the distemper virus will usually continue to experience symptoms or signs of the disease throughout their remaining lifespan, including *"hard pad disease"* as well as *"enamel hypoplasia"*, which is damage to the enamel of the puppy's teeth that are not yet formed or that have not yet pushed through the gums. Enamel hypoplasia is caused by the distemper virus killing the cells that manufacture tooth enamel.

c) Adenovirus

Is a virus that causes infectious canine hepatitis, which can range in severity from very mild to very serious, and can sometimes cause death.

Symptoms can include coughing, loss of appetite, increased thirst and urination, tiredness, runny eyes and nose, vomiting, bruising or bleeding under the skin, swelling of the head, neck and trunk, fluid accumulation in the abdomen area, jaundice (yellow tinge to the skin), a bluish clouding of the cornea of the eye (called "hepatitis blue eye") and seizures.

There is no specific treatment for infectious canine hepatitis, therefore, treatment of this disease is focused on managing symptoms, while the virus runs its course. Hospitalization and intravenous fluid therapy may be required in severe cases.

d) Canine Parainfluenza Virus (CPiV)

The canine parainfluenza virus, also referred to as *"canine influenza virus"*, *"greyhound disease"* and *"race flu"*, which is easily spread through the air or by coming into contact with respiratory secretions, originally only affected horses.

This disease is believed to have adapted to become contagious to dogs and is easily spread from dog to dog, causing symptoms that may become fatal.

While the more frequent occurrences of this respiratory infection are seen in areas with high dog populations, such as race tracks, boarding kennels and pet stores, this virus is highly contagious to any dog or puppy, at any age.

Symptoms can include a dry, hacking cough, difficulty breathing, wheezing, runny nose and eyes, sneezing, fever, loss of appetite, tiredness, depression and possible pneumonia.

In cases where only a cough exists, tests will be required to determine whether the cause of the cough is the parainfluenza virus or the less serious *"kennel cough"*.

While many dogs can naturally recover from this virus, they will remain contagious, and for this reason, in order to prevent the spread to other animals, aggressive treatment of the virus with antibiotics and antiviral drugs will be the general course of action.

In more severe cases, a cough suppressant may be prescribed, as well as intravenous fluids to help prevent secondary bacterial infection.

e) Canine Parvovirus (CPV)

Canine parvovirus is a highly contagious viral illness affecting puppies and dogs. Parvovirus also affects other canine species including foxes, coyotes and wolves.

There are two forms of this virus (1) the more common intestinal form, and (2) the less common cardiac form, which can cause death in young puppies.

Symptoms of the intestinal form of parvovirus include vomiting, bloody diarrhea, weight loss, and lack of appetite, while the less common cardiac form attacks the heart muscle.

Early vaccination in young puppies has radically reduced the incidence of canine parvovirus infection, which is easily transmitted either by direct contact with an infected dog, or indirectly, by sniffing an infected dog's excrement.

The virus can also be brought into a dog's environment on the bottom of human shoes and there is evidence that this hardy virus can live in ground soil for up to a year.

Recovery from parvovirus requires both aggressive and early treatment. With proper treatment, death rates are relatively low (between 5 and 20%), although chances of survival for puppies are much lower than older dogs, and in all instances, there is no guarantee of survival.

Treatment of parvovirus requires hospitalization where intravenous fluids and nutrients are administered to help combat dehydration. As well, antibiotics will be given to counteract secondary bacterial infections, and as necessary, medications to control nausea and vomiting may also be given.

Without prompt and proper treatment, dogs that have severe parvovirus infections can die within 48 to 72 hours.

f) Rabies Vaccinations

Rabies is a viral disease transmitted in the saliva of an infected animal, usually through a bite. The virus travels to the brain along the nerves and once symptoms develop, death is almost certainly inevitable, usually following a prolonged period of suffering.

If you plan to travel out of State or across country borders, you will need to make sure that your Morkie has an up to date Rabies Vaccination Certificate (NASPHV form 51) indicating they have been inoculated against rabies.

Rabies vaccinations for dogs are also compulsory in most countries in mainland Europe, as is permanent identification and registration of dogs through the use of a Pet Passport.

Those living in a country that is rabies free (UK, Eire) are not required to vaccinate their dogs against rabies, unless they intend to travel.

g) Leishmaniasis

Leishmaniasis is caused by a parasite and is transmitted by a bite from a sand fly. There is no definitive answer for effectively combating leishmaniasis, especially since one vaccine will not prevent the known multiple species.

In areas where the known cause is a sandfly, deltamethrin collars (containing a neurotoxic insecticide) worn by the dogs has been proven to be 86% effective.

There are two types of Leishmaniasis: (1) a skin reaction causing hair loss, lesions and ulcerative dermatitis, and (2) a more severe, abdominal organ reaction, which is also known as black fever. When the disease affects organs of the abdominal cavity the symptoms include:

- loss of appetite
- diarrhea
- severe weight loss
- exercise intolerance
- vomiting
- nose bleed

- tarry waste
- fever
- pain in the joints
- excessive thirst and urination
- inflammation of the muscles

Leishmaniasis spreads throughout the body to most organs, with kidney failure being the most common cause of death. Virtually all infected dogs develop this system wide disease and as much as 90% of those infected will also display skin reactions.

Affected dogs in the US are frequently found to have acquired this infection in another country.

Notably, this disease is regularly found in the Middle East, the area around the Mediterranean basin, Portugal, Spain, Africa, South and Central America, southern Mexico and the US (regular cases reported in Oklahoma and Ohio), where it is found in 20 to 40% of the dog population.

There have also been a few reported cases in Switzerland, northern France and the Netherlands.

NOTE: Leishmaniasis is a *"zoonotic"* infection, which is a contagious disease that can be spread between animals and humans. Organisms residing in the Leishmaniasis lesions can be communicated to humans.

Treatment in dogs is often difficult with relapses and Leishmaniasis poses a significant risk to the health of your dog, especially if you travel to the Mediterranean.

h) Lyme's Disease

This is one of the most common tick-borne diseases in the world, which is transmitted by Borrelia bacteria found in the deer or sheep tick.

Lyme's disease, also called *"borreliosis"*, can affect both humans and dogs and this disease can be fatal.

The Borrelia bacteria that causes Lyme's disease, is transmitted by slow-feeding, hard-shelled deer or sheep ticks, and the tick usually has to be attached to the dog for a minimum of 18 hours before the infection is transmitted.

Symptoms of this disease in a young or adult dog include:

- recurrent lameness from joint inflammation
- lack of appetite
- depression
- stiff walk with arched back
- sensitivity to touch
- swollen lymph nodes
- fever
- damage to the kidney
- rare heart or nervous system complications

While Lyme's disease has been reported in dogs throughout the United States and Europe, it is most prevalent in the upper Midwestern states, the Atlantic seaboard, and the Pacific coastal states.

In order to properly diagnose and treat Lyme's disease, blood tests will be required, and if the tests are positive, oral antibiotics will be prescribed to treat the conditions.

Prevention is the key to keeping this disease under control because dogs that have had Lyme disease before are still able to get the disease again.

There is a vaccine for Lyme disease and dogs living in areas that have easy access to these ticks should be vaccinated yearly.

i) Rocky Mountain Spotted Fever (RMSF)

This tick-transmitted disease is very often seen in dogs in the East, Midwest, and plains region of the US, and the organisms causing RMSF are transmitted by both the American dog tick and the Rocky Mountain spotted fever tick, which must be attached to the dog for a minimum of five hours in order to transmit the disease.

Common symptoms of RMSF include:

- fever
- reduced appetite
- depression
- pain in the joints
- lameness
- vomiting
- diarrhea

Some dogs affected with RMSF may develop heart abnormalities, pneumonia, kidney failure, liver damage, or even neurological signs, such an seizures or stumbling gait.

Blood testing will be required to diagnose this disease after which oral antibiotics will be given to treat the infection for approximately two weeks.

Dogs that can clear the organism from their systems will recover and thereafter remain immune to future infection.

j) Ehrlichiosis

This is another tick disease transmitted by both the brown dog tick and the Lone Star Tick.

Ehrlichiosis has been reported in every state in the US, as well as worldwide.

Common symptoms include:

- depression
- reduced appetite
- fever
- stiff and painful joints
- bruising

Signs of infection typically occur less than a month after a tick bite and last for approximately four weeks. There is no vaccine available.

Blood tests may be needed to test for antibodies and treatment requires antibiotics for up to four weeks in order to completely clear the organism.

After a dog has been previously infected, they may develop antibodies to the organism, but will not be immune to reinfection.

Dogs living in areas of the country where this tick disease is common, or widespread, may be prescribed low doses of antibiotics during tick season.

k) Anaplasmosis

Deer ticks and western black-legged ticks are carriers of the bacteria that transmits canine anaplasmosis.

However, there is another form of anaplasmosis (caused by a different bacteria) that is carried by the brown dog tick. Because the deer tick also carries other diseases, some animals may be at risk for developing more than one tick-borne disease at the same time.

Signs of anaplasmosis are similar to ehrlichiosis and include painful joints, diarrhea, fever, and vomiting as well as possible nervous system disorders.

A dog will usually begin to show signs of anaplasmosis within a couple of weeks after infection and diagnosis will require blood and urine testing, and sometimes other specialized laboratory tests.

Treatment is with oral antibiotics for up to 30 days, depending on how severe the infection may be. When this disease is quickly treated, most dogs will recover completely, however, subsequent immunity is not guaranteed, which means that a dog may be reinfected if exposed again.

l) Tick Paralysis

Tick paralysis is caused when ticks secrete a toxin that affects the nervous system. Affected dogs show signs of weakness and limpness approximately one week after being first bitten by ticks.
Symptoms usual begin with a change in pitch of the dog's usual bark, which will become softer, and weakness in the

rear legs that eventually involves all four legs, which is then followed by the dog showing difficulty breathing and swallowing. If the condition is not diagnosed and treated, death can occur.

Treatment involves locating and removing the tick and treatment with tick anti-serum.

m) Canine Coronavirus

While this highly contagious intestinal disease, which is spread through the feces of contaminated dogs, was first discovered in Germany during 1971 when there was an outbreak in sentry dogs, it is now found worldwide.

This virus can be destroyed by most commonly available disinfectants, and symptoms include:

- diarrhea
- vomiting
- weight loss or anorexia

While deaths from this disease are rare, and treatment generally requires only medication to relieve the diarrhea, dogs that are more severely affected may require intravenous fluids to combat dehydration.

There is a vaccine available, which is usually given to puppies, who are more susceptible at a young age, and to show dogs that have a higher risk of exposure to the disease.

n) Leptosporosis

This is a disease that occurs throughout the world that can affect many different kinds of animals, including dogs. The disease is always present in the environment, which makes it easy for any dog to pick up. This is because it is found in rats, and wildlife, as well as domestic livestock.

Veterinarians see more cases in the late summer and fall – probably because that is when pets and wildlife are out and about, and more cases also occur after heavy rainfalls.

The disease is most common in mild or tropical climates around the World, and in the US or Canada, it is more common in states or provinces that have heavy rainfall.

Cold winter conditions lower the risk because leptospira do not tolerate the freezing and thawing of near-zero temperatures. They are killed rapidly by drying, but they persist in standing water, dampness, mud and alkaline conditions.

Most of the infected wild animals and domestic animals that spread leptospirosis do not appear ill.

The leptospira take up residence in the kidneys of infected animals, which can include rats, mice, skunks, and raccoons and when these animals void urine, they contaminate their environment with living leptospira.

While dogs usually become infected by sniffing this urine or by wading, swimming in or drinking contaminated water, and this is how the disease passes from animal to animal, the leptospira can also enter through a bite wound or by dogs eating infected material.

o) Additional Vaccinations

Depending upon where you and your Morkie live, your veterinarian may suggest additional vaccinations to help combat diseases that may be more common in your area.

p) When Is a Puppy Vaccinated?

The first vaccination needle is normally given to a puppy around six to eight weeks of age, which means that generally, it will be the responsibility of the Morkie breeder to ensure that the puppy's first shots have been received before their new owner takes them home.

Then it will be the new Morkie puppy's guardians that will be responsible for ensuring that the next two sets of shots, which are usually given three to four weeks after each other, are given by the new guardian's veterinarian at the proper intervals.

4. De-Worming

De-worming kills internal parasites that your dog/puppy may have.

Note: no matter how sanitary your conditions, or where you live, your dog will have internal parasites, because it is not a matter of cleanliness.

It is recommended by the Center for Disease Control (CDC) that puppies be dewormed every 2 weeks, until they are 3 months old, and then every month after that, in order to control worms.

Many vets recommend worming dogs for tapeworm and roundworms every 6-12 months.

5. Tail Docking

Tail docking, also referred to as tail shortening or bobbing to reduce the length of a dog's natural tail length has come to be a hot subject of discussion, with many believing that the method, which was originally executed for efficient health and wellness associated factors, ought to be banned for all breeds.

With respect to the Morkie cross breed, some breeders will dock the tails, especially the ones that look more like the Yorkshire Terrier, while others will leave their natural length, which will curl up over the dog's back, like the Maltese.

When the Yorkshire Terrier was a hunting dog, it made good sense to dock their tails, since they were pursuing rats and various other burrowing animals that stay in tunnels and docking their tails avoided the tail from becoming damaged or harmed in tight spaces.

Nowadays, docking or shortening the tail has come to be absolutely nothing more than an aesthetic enhancement.

a) Non-Surgical Docking

When a young puppy is a few days old, docking the tail is an easy procedure that includes limiting circulation to the tail by firmly banding the tail by connecting a rubber ligature around the puppy's tail very soon after it's born.

Positioning a band around the tail restricts blood circulation to the end of the tail, which causes the tail to fall off within a number of days.

b) Surgical Docking

The procedure for reducing or shortening the top section of an older new puppy's or dog's tail needs to be performed by an accredited veterinarian specialist and as this treatment will certainly be a lot more painful for an older puppy or dog, they should be fully anesthetized.

6. Special Care When Pregnant

As pregnancy only lasts nine weeks, and a Morkie female will go into labor within 56 to 66 days after becoming pregnant, a pregnant Morkie will require immediate attention when the first signs of pregnancy appear.

Immediately upon noticing signs of pregnancy you will want to take your Morkie to the veterinarian to confirm the pregnancy and to receive instructions for the proper feeding and care.

During the first days of pregnancy, your Morkie may experience morning sickness.

Your veterinarian may recommend increasing food intake or adding an egg or cottage cheese to your Morkie's meals and switching to puppy kibble, which is higher in protein, at around the 30 day mark.

As the Morkie female becomes heavier with the puppies, she will lose interest in exercising and her other normal activities and will need to sleep more.

When the time for birthing is drawing near, the Morkie female will start to display "nesting" characteristics, where she will search for a warm and safe place to give birth.

You can help by providing a nesting box and she will likely want to take things into the box to make it more comfortable, such as towels or even a stuffed toy that she will begin to mother.

When the time draws near to whelping, the Morkie female may completely lose her appetite and show distress by pacing, panting, and acting uncomfortable.

Her temperature needs to be checked, and should be around 100.2 to 100.8 degrees Fahrenheit (37.89 to 38.22 degrees Centigrade), and when it drops to approximately 98 to 99.4 degrees Fahrenheit (36.67 to 37.44 degrees Centigrade), the puppies will usually be born within 24 hours.

If you are at all worried about the birthing process you will want to take the mother Morkie immediately to your veterinarian's office.

If all goes well at home, within 5-6 hours of the last puppy's birth, you will need to take the Morkie female and her puppies to your veterinarian for a check up to ensure that the female has not retained any puppies or placentas and that the puppies are all in good health.

7. Licensing

Many cities and jurisdictions around the world require that dogs be licensed.

Usually a dog license is an identifying tag that the dog will be required to wear on their collar. The tag will have an identifying number and a contact number for the registering organization, so that if someone finds a lost dog wearing a tag, the owner of the dog can be contacted.

Most dog tags are only valid for one year, and will need to be renewed annually at the beginning of every New Year, which involves paying a fee that can vary from jurisdiction to jurisdiction.

For instance, owners of dogs living in Bejing, China must pay a licensing fee of $600. (£360), while licensing for dogs living in Great Britain was abolished in 1987.

Ireland and Northern Ireland both require dogs to be licensed and in Germany dog ownership is taxed, rather than requiring licensing, with higher taxes being paid for breeds of dogs deemed to be "dangerous".

Most US states and municipalities have licensing laws in effect and Canadian, Australian and New Zealand dogs must also be licensed, with the yearly cost approximately $30 to $50 (£18 to £30) depending upon whether the dog is spayed or neutered.

8. Pet Insurance

A common question pet guardians ask themselves when considering medical insurance for their dog is whether they can afford <u>not</u> to have it.

In light of all the new treatments and medications that are now available for our dogs, that usually come with a very high price tag, an increasing number of guardians have decided to add pet insurance to their list of monthly expenses.

On the other hand, other humans believe that placing money into a savings account, in case unforeseen medical treatments are required, makes more sense.

Pet insurance coverage can cost anywhere from $2,000 to $6,000 USD (£1201 to £3604) over an average lifespan, and unless your dog is involved in a serious accident, you may never need to pay out that much for treatment.

Whether you decide to start a savings account for your Morkie so that you will always have funds available for unforeseen health issues, or you decide to buy a health insurance plan, most of us dog lovers will go to any lengths to save the life of our beloved companions.

For those humans who may not be independently wealthy, having some sort of pet insurance will provide peace of mind that could be much more preferable than the extra stress involved in going into debt should you be faced with a substantial veterinarian bill.

Keep in mind that veterinary science has advanced in recent years, which means that veterinarians and our canine companions now have access to sophisticated, yet very costly diagnostic equipment.

Having access to advanced technological tools and procedures means that our dogs are now being offered treatment options that were once only reserved for humans. Now, some canine conditions that were once considered fatal are being treated at considerable costs ranging anywhere from $1,000. to $5,000. (£597 to £2,986) or more.

However, even in the face of rapidly increasing costs of caring for our dogs, owners purchasing pet insurance remain a small minority.

In an effort to increase the numbers of people buying pet insurance, insurers have teamed with the American Kennel Club and Petco Animal Supplies to offer the insurance, and more than 1,600 companies, such as Office Depot and Google, offer pet insurance coverage to their employees as an optional employee benefit.

Even though you might believe that pet insurance will be your savior anytime your dog needs a trip to the vet's office, you really need to be careful when considering an insurance plan, because there are many policies that contain small print that excludes certain ages, hereditary or chronic conditions.

Unfortunately, most people don't consider pet insurance when their pets are healthy, because buying pet insurance means playing the odds, and unless your dog becomes seriously ill, you end up paying for something that may never happen.

However, just like automobile insurance, you can't buy it after you've had that accident.

Therefore, since many of us in today's uncertain economy could not afford to pay a high veterinarian bill, generally speaking, the alternative of paying monthly pet insurance premiums will provide peace of mind and provide better veterinarian care for our best friends.

The right policy can be an asset to the health care of your dog while having a significant impact on reducing the cost you might have to pay as a result of an emergency visit to your veterinarian's office.

Shop around, because as with all insurance policies, pet insurance policies will vary greatly between companies and the only way to know for sure exactly what sort of coverage you are buying is to have a copy of that policy in front of you so that you can clearly see what will be covered and what will not be covered.

Don't forget to carefully read the fine print to avoid any nasty surprises, because the time to discover that a certain procedure will not be covered is not when you are in the middle of filing a claim.

Before Purchasing a Policy

There are several considerations to be aware of before choosing to purchase a pet insurance policy, including:

- Is your dog required to undergo a physical exam?
- Is there a waiting period before the policy becomes active?

- What percentage of the bill does the insurance company pay — after the deductible?
- Are payments limited or capped in any way?
- Are there co-pays (cost to you up front)?
- Does the plan cover pre-existing conditions?
- Does the plan cover chronic or recurring medical problems?
- Can you choose any vet or animal hospital to treat your pet?
- Are prescription medications covered?
- Are you covered when traveling with your pet?
- Does the policy pay if your pet is being treated and then dies?

When you love your dog and worry that you may not have the funds to cover an emergency medical situation that could unexpectedly cost thousands, the right pet insurance policy will provide both peace of mind and better health care for your beloved fur friend.

9. Yearly Cost of Owning a Morkie

Although it is impossible to accurately estimate what the cost of owning every Morkie might be, because unexpected medical problems might arise that would not otherwise be considered average, it's important to consider more than just the daily cost of feeding your Morkie.

Many humans do not think about whether or not they can truly afford to care for a dog before they bring one home, and not being prepared can cause stress and problems later on.

Remember that being financially responsible for your Morkie is a large part of being a good guardian.

Beyond the initial investment of purchasing your Morkie puppy from a reputable breeder, for most guardians, owning a Morkie will include the costs associated with the following:

- food
- treats
- pee pads, poop bags, potty patches
- leashes and collars
- safety harnesses
- travel kennels or bags
- house training pens
- clothing
- toys
- beds
- grooming
- regular veterinary care
- obedience or dog whispering classes
- pet sitting, walking or boarding
- pet insurance
- yearly licensing
- unexpected emergencies

As you can see, depending upon where you shop, what type of food you feed your Morkie, what sort of veterinarian or grooming care you choose, whether or not you have pet insurance and what types of items you purchase for your Morkie's well being, the yearly cost of owning a Morkie could be estimated at anywhere between $700 and $3,000 (£420 and £1,800) per year.

Other contributing factors that may have an effect on the overall yearly cost of owning a Morkie can include the region where you live, the accessibility of the items you need, your own lifestyle and your Morkie's age and individual needs.

Chapter 7: Health Problems

1. Common Problems

The most common issues seen with Morkies are eye, ear and dental health problems, discussed in Chapter 10.

2. Congenital Defects

Congenital defects refer to abnormalities of the body that are present when the Morkie puppy is born. These types of defects may involve any part of the puppy's body or any system or organ within the puppy's body.

Some congenital defects can be slight or minor and may naturally resolve themselves as the puppy grows, while others defects can cause or prevent the normal development and function of the puppy, even to the point of causing early death.

Certain genetic predispositions that have been found to occur in the Yorkshire Terrier breed and the Maltese breed, may also be prevalent when mixing the two together in the Morkie hybrid.

The more common congenital defects may include:

a) Hypoglycemia

Hypoglycemia, or low blood sugar, is usually seen in very young puppies (5-16 weeks of age) and is a result of a puppy not eating regular meals throughout the day.

Very small Morkie puppies may be especially prone to hypoglycemia because their insufficient muscle mass makes it difficult for them to store glucose and regulate blood sugar.

Symptoms of hypoglycemia include drowsiness, listlessness, a glassy-eyed look, and shaky or uncoordinated movement when walking because the the brain relies upon sugar to function properly.

The gums of a Morkie puppy suffering from low blood sugar will appear very pale or grey in color and once the gums have become pale the puppy may require force feeding and injection of fluids as they may also be dehydrated. In extreme cases of hypoglycemia, the puppy may have a seizure or go into a coma.

A Morkie puppy or dog displaying any of these symptoms should be immediately given sugar in the form of corn syrup or honey and emergency veterinary treatment in order to avoid permanent brain damage or even death.

Sometimes a young Morkie puppy can get very busy playing and will forget to eat, which can result in a sudden drop in blood sugar.

If you are not paying attention to how much your Morkie is eating, and even if you are, it is a good idea to keep on hand a tube of high calorie paste that can be used in an emergency to get blood sugar quickly back to normal levels.

b) Luxating Patella

This slipping or floating kneecap condition is a common defect seen in many smaller breeds, including the Morkie, and may also be caused by accidentally falling or jumping from a height.

Usually, the condition will present itself between the ages of 4 and 6 months.

Often you will see a dog with this problem appear to be skipping down the road as they occasionally lift one leg as the kneecap slips out of the patellar groove and the leg locks up. In more severe cases, surgery may be the recommended treatment option to correct this condition.

c) Portosystemic Shunt (PSS)

This life-threatening, abnormal circulating of the blood is a serious congenital condition, also called *"liver shunt"*, and is a malformation of the portal vein that transports blood to the liver for cleansing.

If not treated, PSS will lead to seizures, blindness, coma and death. In this condition, some of the dog's blood bypasses the liver, which means that this blood is not cleansed of harmful toxins before it returns to poison the heart and other vital organs. PSS results in toxic effects on the brain as well as other body organs.

A Morkie suffering from PSS may display a wide variety of symptoms, including small size, poor appetite, weak muscles, learning difficulty, poor coordination, vomiting, diarrhea, and behavioral problems.

Unless PSS can be successfully treated (which is difficult and not always possible), the affected dog will suffer from progressive dementia due to brain damage that will lead to coma and eventual death.

It is possible to test puppies for PSS using a bile acid stimulation test, which can be done at a young age, before a puppy is sold by a breeder.

Treatment of PSS begins with stabilization through medical management to improve the dog's health, consisting of feeding a low protein diet combined with oral administration of antibiotics and lactulose.

Medical treatment will decrease the amount of bacteria in the intestines, which will then minimize the production of toxins.

The next step in treatment will be surgery, which involves surgical narrowing or complete tying off of the abnormal shunt vessel, which can be a very difficult surgery.

Prognosis is good if the dog survives without succumbing to seizure within the first 1-2 days after surgery.

c) Tracheal Collapse

Tracheal collapse is an airway obstruction of the trachea, or *"windpipe,"* sometimes also referred to as *"reverse sneezing"*.

The trachea is a tube made up of sturdy rings of cartilage through which air is transported in and out of the dog's lungs. As air is squeezed through the windpipe during breathing, sometimes the tracheal rings collapse, which causes a coughing or honking sound.

Usually this coughing or honking is brought on by excitement over visiting a new dog or eating an especially tasty treat. Sometimes the symptoms may be provoked by irritants in the environment, such as vehicle exhaust, smoke or dust.

Further, symptoms can be exacerbated when exercising during hot or humid weather, and more so if the dog is overweight.

This genetic condition primarily affects toy breeds of both sexes, and the while the symptoms of collapsing trachea can manifest at any age, on average, signs begin to appear when the dog is is six to seven years of age.

Although treatment, which usually consists of cough suppressants and antibiotics, will not cure the condition, a study released in 1994 indicated that 71% of dogs treated showed a good long-term response.

In mild cases, a honking or coughing session will only last for a few seconds and can be assisted by gently rubbing the dog's nose or giving a quick squeeze around the rib cage to help relax the trachea and get the air flowing again.

In severe cases, surgery is recommended, which involves applying prosthetic rings to the outside of the trachea. The success rate of this tricky operation is reported to be in the 75- to 85% range.

3. Teacupism

While our human society seems completely enthralled with everything small, breeding ever smaller sized Morkies is not a particularly good idea for the dog, because in order to breed smaller, it means breeding runts with runts, which generally produces weaker puppies with more health problems.

"Teacupism" is a term used to describe abnormally small, or "teacup" sized dogs, including the Morkie. Any dog weighing less than 4 pounds when fully grown is considered to be teacup sized.

"Teacupism" is a highly controversial breeding practice that is not encouraged by responsible breeders because it creates weak dogs with many health problems, including shortened lifespans.

Undersized Morkies will generally live a much shorter life because they are especially prone to health problems such as chronic diarrhea and vomiting.

Very small Morkies will be more sensitive to anesthesia and are much more difficult to operate on for spaying or neutering as their organs are so tiny.

As well, a very tiny Morkie can be more easily injured, sometimes even breaking their legs simply from jumping off of a chair.

Fragility

Many people do not realize how incredibly fragile a toy breed can be, and when breeders specifically shrink the size of a toy breed ever further, the dog becomes that much more fragile.

For instance, a human can seriously injure or kill a small Morkie by stepping on them or by accidentally sitting on them.

As well, a tiny but feisty little Morkie could easily injure or even kill themselves by fearlessly leaping out of your arms.

Further, many larger dogs with a high prey drive may think that such a small dog is a rodent, and they can quickly grab a small Morkie and kill them or break their neck with one quick shake.

Owning a very small toy breed, such as a teacup Morkie will mean that you must be constantly vigilant and keep your dog under close supervision so that you are aware of everything that is happening and can avoid potentially harmful situations.

Very small Morkies with fearless temperaments need to be kept on leash because they may place themselves into all sorts of circumstances whereby they could easily be injured if they are not under your complete control.

As well, a very small Morkie can easily be carried off by large birds of prey, such as hawks, eagles or owls.

A teacup sized Morkie will NOT be a suitable pet for young children, who may accidentally hurt them by squeezing too tightly, dropping them, or stepping on them.

Children are usually loud, fast moving, boisterous and often clumsy, which is a combination for danger around a small dog who might suffer all manner of injuries at the hands of a young child.

Finally, teacup sized dogs often feel overwhelmed simply because everything around them is so much larger and they may develop nervous habits, fear and stress that may manifest itself with constant trembling and/or defensive biting.

Chapter 8: Temperament

The Morkie is a small or *"toy"* breed that never lets their small size deter them from taking a head on approach to all that life has to offer.

What the Morkie may lack in size, they certainly make up for with their feisty and energetic attitude, and if the family members do not provide rules and boundaries, this little dog will soon take over as ruler of the roost.

Early, consistent and ongoing training is very important in order to help the Morkie understand that the human family members are top dogs and that it is their place to be an obedient follower.

The Morkie likes to be glued to their guardians and will enjoy nothing more than curling up on a warm lap.

They also enjoy a warm and cozy bed to sleep in, and while many guardians will allow their Morkie companions to sleep in bed with them, this is not a very safe or particularly good idea, because this tiny dog could accidentally get crushed by a human.

Also, allowing your dog to sleep in your bed sends confusing messages about who is the boss in the human/canine relationship.

The best situation is to provide your Morkie with a warm and cozy bed or kennel in your bedroom and to begin teaching them at a young age, that this is where they sleep at nighttime.

While the Morkie will get along well with other dogs and pets that they are raised with or properly introduced to, they are affectionate and loving little dogs who will bond very closely with human family members and will NOT do well if left along for long periods of time.

A Morkie left alone will become bored, lonely and distraught which will likely lead to destructive chewing or other unwanted behavior as well as non-stop barking as they vocalize their unhappiness.

1. Behavior With Children and Pets

Prospective Morkie owners with children need to keep in mind that while the Morkie is an energetic and entertaining little dog, it is also a toy breed, which means that it can be somewhat fragile.

Play sessions with young children should be supervised to ensure that the Morkie is not roughly treated, that it does not get too tightly squeezed, stepped on, dropped or somehow become accidentally injured.

As well, the Morkie can become snappish with younger children who do not respect the dog's boundaries, therefore, caution and supervision when introducing small, or overly excited children needs to be exercised so that the Morkie does not feel that it needs to protect itself.

When introducing a Morkie to larger dogs, a guardian will need to be aware that the fearless little Morkie will often not know their place or be at all intimidated by the larger dog, and if allowed to be protective of it's owner or family members, may charge and bark at a larger dog. This type of jealous or protective behavior must never be permitted because the tiny Morkie is at a distinct disadvantage should a larger dog decide to fight back.

The Morkie can be a vocal watch dog, who will bark when they hear a new person entering the home, however, they will usually become quickly social and friendly as soon as they realize that the person is a friend.

2. Is the Morkie an Escape Artist?

Keep in mind that both the Maltese and the feisty Yorkshire Terrier were designed to hunt rodents in the marshlands, or dig into the ground to retrieve them, therefore they may have a natural tendency for hunting rodents and/or digging their way out of yards.

Since they are so small in size, any tiny opening in a fence will be an open door invitation to a curious Morkie who has caught a scent or simply has a zest for adventure.

Early spaying or neutering of a Morkie puppy will go a long way toward helping to curb any wanderlust tendencies.

Chapter 9: Coat Colors and Types

The Maltese is a pure white dog and the breed standard acceptable coat colors for the Yorkshire Terrier are black and tan, black and gold, blue and gold, or blue and tan, which means that breeding these two together will produce a Morkie coat in a wide variety of color combinations.

The Morkie coat can be any unique color combination of black, brown, white or beige, or can be a solid color with markings of other colors.

1. Puppy Coats

A Morkie puppy coat will be darker when they are first born and soft to the touch and although may drastically change color from puppy to adult, will usually remain soft or silky.

By the time the Morkie puppy is approximately five or six months old, they will have grown in their adult coat

2. Adult Coats

While both parent breeds of the Morkie have long coats that continue to grow throughout their lives, the texture of each breed's coat is quite different, and a Morkie puppy may inherit one or the other coat type, or a coat that is a combination of the two.

No matter which type of coat a Morkie puppy inherits, they will always require regular brushing, bathing and trimming to keep the coat in good condition.

Many Morkies have apricot, white, or brown coat coloring with the most common coat color for a Morkie being the black and tan (inherited from the Yorkshire Terrier), which later in life fades to a silver grayish color.

3. Coat Types

a) Silky

A Morkie puppy may have a coat that is more like the Yorkshire Terrier, who has a silkier coat.

b) Cottony

A Morkie puppy may have a coat that is more like the Maltese, who has a cotton-like texture that tends to malt more frequently.

4. Defining Features

When breeding the Yorkshire Terrier with the Maltese, the Morkie will have a similar body size and structure, however, the Yorkshire Terrier's coloring seems to be the most dominant.

This means that a larger percentage of Morkie puppies will look more like their Yorkie parent.

However, puppies that are born white tend to naturally favor the Maltese parent.

As the ears on the parent breeds are quite different, a Morkie puppy can be born with either upright ears, or folded drop-ears or partially upright but folded over on the tips.

Whether or not the Morkie tail is docked or shortened at birth, the tails are usually naturally quite short.

Chapter 10: Grooming

It will be very important to get your Morkie puppy used to the routine of grooming early on, so that they will not be traumatized for the rest of their life, every time grooming is necessary.

Not taking the time to regularly involve your Morkie puppy in grooming sessions could lead to serious, unwanted behavior that may include trauma to your dog, not to mention stress or injury to you in the form of biting and scratching, that could result in a lifetime of unhappy grooming sessions.

When you neglect regular, daily or at least a weekly at home grooming session with your puppy or dog to remove tangles and keep mats to a minimum, this will not only cost you and your canine companion, in terms of possible trauma and extended time on the grooming table, it will cost you a higher fee should you opt to have regular clipping and grooming carried out at a professional salon.

An effective home regimen will include not just surface brushing, but also getting to all those sensitive areas easily missed around the ears and collar area, the armpit area, and the back end and tail.

Do not allow yourself to get caught in the *"my dog doesn't like it"* trap which is an excuse many owners will use to avoid regular grooming sessions.

When you allow your dog to dictate whether they will permit a grooming session, you are setting a dangerous precedent that could lead to lifetime of trauma for both you and your Morkie.

When humans neglect daily grooming routines, many dogs develop a heightened sensitivity, especially with regard to having their legs and feet held, touched, brushed or clipped and will do anything they can to avoid the process when you need to groom them.

Make a pact with yourself right from the first day you bring your puppy home, never to neglect a regular grooming routine and not to avoid sensitive areas, such as trimming toenails, just because your dog may not particular *"like"* it.

1. Bath Time

Step One: before you get your Morkie anywhere near the water, it's important to make sure that you brush out any debris, knots or tangles from their coat before you begin the bathing process because getting knots or tangles wet could make them tighter and much more difficult to remove, which will cause your dog pain and distress.

As well, removing any debris from your dog's coat beforehand, including dead undercoat and shedding hair will make the entire process easier on both you, your dog, and your drains, which will become clogged with hair if you don't remove it beforehand.

Step Two: if your Morkie has a long coat, the process will be much easier if you first spray the coat with a light mist of leave-in conditioner before brushing. This will also help to protect the delicate hair strands from breaking.

Step Three: whether you're bathing your Morkie in your kitchen sink or your bathtub, you will always want to first lay down a rubber bath mat to provide a more secure footing for your dog and to prevent your sink or tub from being scratched.

Step Four: have everything you need for the bath (shampoo, conditioner, sponge, towels) right next to the sink or tub, so you don't have to go searching once your dog is already in the water. Place cotton balls in your Morkie's ear canals to prevent accidental splashes from entering the ear canal.

Step Five: fill the tub or sink with four to six inches of lukewarm water (not too hot as dogs are more sensitive to hot water than us humans) and put your Morkie in the water. Completely wet your dog's coat right down to the skin by using a detachable shower head. If you don't have a spray attachment, a cup or pitcher will work just as well.

TIP: no dog likes to have water poured over its head and into it's eyes, so use a wet sponge or wash cloth to wet the head area.

Step Six: apply shampoo as indicated on the bottle instructions by beginning at the head and working your way down the back. Be careful not to get shampoo in the eyes, nose, mouth or ears. Comb the shampoo lather through your dog's hair with your fingers, making sure you don't miss the areas under the legs and tail.

Step Seven: after allowing the shampoo to remain in your dog's coat for a couple of minutes, thoroughly rinse your Morkie's coat, right down to the skin with clean, lukewarm water using the spray attachment, cup or pitcher. Comb through your dog's coat with your fingers to make sure all shampoo residue has been rinsed away.

TIP: shampoo remaining in a dog's coat will lead to irritation and itching. Once you've rinsed, take the time to rinse again, especially in the armpits and underneath the tail area.

Use your hands to gently squeeze all excess water from your dog's coat.

Step Eight: apply conditioner as indicated on the bottle instructions and work the conditioner throughout your Morkie's coat. Leave the conditioner in your dog's coat for two minutes and then thoroughly rinse the conditioner out of your dog's coat with warm water, unless the conditioner you are using is a "leave-in", no-rinse formula.

Pull the plug on your sink or tub and let the water drain away as you use your hands to squeeze excess water from your Morkie's legs and feet.

Step Nine: immediately out of the water, wrap your Morkie in dry towels so they don't get cold and use the towels to gently squeeze out extra water before you allow them a water spraying shake. If your dog has long hair, do not rub your dog with the towels, as this will create tangles and breakage in the long hair.

NOTE: if your dog has a short or shaved coat, you will not need to be so particular and in this case may massage the shampoo or conditioner in circular motions through the coat and can rub them down a little more with the towels after they are out of the tub.

Dry your Morkie right away with your hand held hairdryer and be careful not to let the hot air get too close to their skin.

TIP: if your Morkie's hair is longer, blow the hair in the direction of growth to help prevent breakage and if the hair is short, you can use your hand or a brush or comb to lift and fluff the hair to help it dry more quickly.

TIP: place your hand between the hairdryer and your Morkie's hair so that they will never get a direct blast of hot air and never blow air directly into their face or ears.

Show Dog Coats

If you have decided to let your Morkie keep a long, flowing coat that reaches the floor, be aware that this type of coat will be much higher maintenance.

Grooming can include weekly bathing and oiling of the coat to make the hair shine and to prevent hair from breaking and at the very least, you will need to provide daily brushing and combing sessions to keep debris out of the longer hair.

Further, you will need to be much more careful when bathing a Morkie with a long, silky coat.

For instance, when you apply the shampoo onto the back, you will not want to rub in circles, but rather use only downward strokes to distribute the suds because washing up and down or massaging in circular motions will tangle and break the fine hair.

2. Clipping

If you have decided to learn how to clip your Morkie's hair yourself, rather than taking them to a professional grooming salon, you will need to purchase all the tools necessary and learn how to properly use them.

The first step will be learning which blades to use in your electric clipper in order to get the length of cut you desire.

The "blade cut" refers to the length of the dog's hair that will remain after cutting against the natural lie of the hair.

As an example, if the blade cut indicates 1/4" (0.6 cm) the length of your Morkie's hair after cutting will be 1/4" (0.6 cm) if you cut with the natural growth of their hair, or it will be 1/8" (0.3 cm) if you cut against the direction of the hair growth.

Even if you decide to leave the full grooming to the professionals, in between grooming sessions you will still need to have a brush, a comb, a small pair of scissors and a pair of nail clippers on hand, so that you can keep the hair clipped away from your Morkie's eyes, knots and tangles out of their coat and their nails trimmed short.

A good quality clipper for a Morkie, such as an *"Andis"*, *"Wahl"* or *"Oster"* professional electric clipper will cost between $100 and $300 (£60 and £180) or more.

3. Ear Care

There are many ear cleaning creams, drops, oils, rinses, solutions and wipes formulated for cleaning your dog's ears that you can purchase from your local pet store or veterinarian's office.

Or you may prefer to use a home remedy that will just as efficiently clean your Morkie's ears, such as Witch Hazel or a 50:50 mixture of hydrogen peroxide and purified water.

Tip: if you are going to make your own ear cleaning solution, find a bottle with a nozzle, measure your solution, properly diluted and mixed into the bottle, and use your preparation to saturate a cloth to wipe out the visible part of your dog's ears. Always make sure the ears are totally dried after cleaning.

4. Eye Care

Although some breeds, like the Morkie, are much more prone to build up of daily eye secretions, every dog should have their eyes regularly wiped with a warm, damp cloth to remove build up of daily secretions in the corners of the eyes.

The Morkie will be prone to a build up of secretions that can be unattractive and uncomfortable for the dog as the hair becomes glued together.

If this build up is not removed every day, it can quickly become a cause of bacterial yeast growth that can lead to eye infections.

When you take a moment every day to gently wipe your dog's eyes with a warm, moist cloth, and keep the hair trimmed away from their eyes, you will help to keep your dog's eyes comfortable and infection free.

5. Nail Care

Allowing your Morkie to have long, untrimmed nails can result in various health hazards including infections or an irregular and uncomfortable gait that can result in damage to their skeleton.

Although most dogs do not particular enjoy the process of having their nails trimmed, and most humans find the exercise to be a little scary, regular nail trimming is a very important grooming practice that should never be overlooked.

In order to keep your Morkie's toenails in good condition and the proper length, you will need to purchase either a guillotine or plier nail trimmer at a pet store and learn how to correctly use it.

NOTE: when your Morkie is a small puppy, it will be best to trim their nails with a pair of nail scissors, which you can purchase at any pet store, that are smaller and easier to use on smaller nails.

Further, if you want your dog's nails to be smooth, without the sharp edges clipping alone can create, you will also want to invest in a toenail file or a special, slow speed, rotary trimmer (Dremel™), designed especially for dog nails. Some dogs will prefer the rotary trimmer to the squeezing sensation of the nail clipper.

NOTE: <u>never</u> use a regular Dremel™ tool on a dog's toenails as it will be too high speed and will burn your dog's toenails. Only use a slow speed Dremel™, Model 7300-PT Pet Nail Grooming Tool.

6. Dental Care

As a conscientious Morkie guardian you will need to regularly care for your dog's teeth throughout their entire life.

a) Retained Primary Teeth

Often times a young dog will not naturally lose their puppy or baby teeth, especially those with small jaws, like the Morkie, without intervention from a licensed veterinarian.

Therefore, keep a close watch on your puppy's teeth around the age of 6 or 7 months of age to make certain that the baby teeth have fallen out and that the adult teeth have space to grown in.

If your Morkie puppy has not naturally lost their baby teeth, they will need to be pulled, in order to allow room for the adult teeth to grow in, and the best time to do this will be at the same time they visit the veterinarian's office to be spayed or neutered.

Smaller dogs, like the Morkie, have a smaller jaw, which can result in more problems with teeth overcrowding.

An overcrowded mouth can cause teeth to grow unevenly or crooked and food and plaque to build up, which will eventually result in bacterial grow on the surface of the teeth, causing bad breath, gum and dental disease.

b) Periodontal Disease

Please be aware that 80% of three year old dogs suffer from periodontal disease and bad breath because their guardians do not look after their dog's teeth.

What makes this shocking statistic even worse is that it is entirely possible to prevent canine gum disease and bad breath.

The pain associated with periodontal disease will make your dog's life miserable, as it will be painful for them to eat and the associated bacteria can infect many parts of the dog's body, including the heart, kidney, liver and brain, all of which they will have to suffer in silence.

If your Morkie has bad breath, this could be the first sign of gum disease caused by plaque build-up on the teeth.

As well, if your Morkie is drooling excessively, this may be a symptom secondary to dental disease. Your dog may be experiencing pain or the salivary glands may be reacting to inflammation from excessive bacteria in the mouth. If you notice your Morkie drooling, you will want to have them professionally examined at your veterinarian's office.

c) Teeth Brushing

Slowly introduce your Morkie to teeth brushing early on in their young life so that they will not fear it.

Begin with a finger cap toothbrush when they are young puppies, and then move to a soft bristled toothbrush, or even an electric brush, as all you have to do is hold it against the teeth while the brush does all the work. Sometimes with a manual brush, you may brush too hard and cause the gums to bleed.

Never use human toothpaste or mouthwash on your dog's teeth because dogs cannot spit and human toothpaste that contains toxic fluoride will be swallowed. There are many flavored dog toothpastes available at the pet store or veterinarian's office.

Also, it's a good idea to get your dog used to the idea of occasionally having their teeth scraped or scaled, especially the back molars which tend to build up plaque. Be very careful if you are doing this yourself because the tools are sharp.

TIP: if you need help keeping your dog's mouth open while you do a quick brush or scrape, get yourself a piece of hard material (rubber or leather) that they can bite down on, so that they cannot fully close their mouth while you work on their teeth.

Get your Morkie used to having it's mouth handled and your fingers rubbing their teeth and gums when they are a young puppy.

Next, buy some canine toothpaste at your local pet store specially flavored to appeal to dogs and apply this to your dog's teeth with your finger.

Then slowly introduce the manual or electric toothbrush to your Morkie. When you go slowly, they will get used to the buzzing of the electric brush, which will do a superior job of cleaning their teeth.

First, let them see the electric brush, then let them hear it buzzing, and before you put it in their mouth, let them feel the buzzing sensation on their body, while you move it slowly toward their head and muzzle.

When your Morkie will allow you to touch their muzzle while the brush is turned on, the next step is to brush a couple of teeth at a time until they get used to having them all brushed at the same time.

Whether you let the electric toothbrush do the work for you, or you are using a manual toothbrush, make certain that you brush in a circular motion with the bristles of the brush angled so that they get underneath the gum line to help prevent gum disease and loose teeth.

d) Teeth Scaling

Use of a tooth scraper once or twice a month can help to remove plaque buildup. Most accumulation will be found on the outside of the teeth and on the back molars, near the gum line. Go slowly and carefully because these tools are sharp and only do this when your dog is calm and relaxed, a little bit at a time.

e) Healthy Teeth Tips

Despite what most dog owners might put up with as normal, it is <u>not</u> normal for your dog to have smelly dog breath or canine halitosis.

Bad breath is the first sign of an unhealthy mouth, which could involve gum disease or tooth decay.

The following tips will help keep your Morkie's mouth and teeth healthy:

- keep your dog's teeth sparkling white and their breath fresh by using old-fashioned hydrogen as your doggy toothpaste (hydrogen peroxide is what's in the human whitening toothpaste). There will be such a small amount on the brush that it will not harm your dog, and will kill any bacteria in your dog's mouth.

- many canine toothpastes are formulated with active enzymes to help keep tartar build-up at bay.

- help prevent tooth plaque and doggy halitosis by feeding your dog natural, hard bones at least once a month, which will also help to remove tartar while polishing and keeping their teeth white.

    Feed large, bones so there is no danger of swallowing, and do NOT boil the bones first because this makes the bone soft (which defeats the purpose of removing plaque), and could cause it to splinter into smaller pieces that could create a choking hazard for your dog.

- small dogs with shorter muzzles, such as the Morkie tend to be more vulnerable to teeth and gum problems, therefore, you really need to be brushing their teeth every single day.

- feed a daily dental chew or hard biscuit to help to remove tartar while exercising jaws and massaging gums. Some dental chews contain natural breath freshening cinnamon, cloves or chlorophyll.

- coconut oil also helps to prevent smelly dog breath while giving your dog's digestive, immune and metabolic functions a boost at the same time. Dogs love the taste, so add a 1/2 tsp to your Morkie's dinner and their breath will soon be much sweeter.

Keep your Morkie's mouth comfortable and healthy by getting into the habit of brushing their teeth every night before bedtime.

7. Skin Care

Keeping your Morkie's coat clean by regularly bathing with canine shampoo and conditioner and free from debris and parasites, as well as providing plenty of clean water and feeding them a high quality diet free from allergy-causing ingredients will go a long way toward keeping their skin healthy and itch-free.

8. Brushing and Combing

Brushing and combing your dog's coat is an often overlooked task that is a necessary part of maintaining your dog's health.

As well, taking time to brush and comb your Morkie's coat will also give you an opportunity to bond with your dog, while identifying any problems (such as lumps or bumps and matted hair) early on, before they may become more serious.

Make sure that your grooming sessions are as pleasant as possible by choosing the right tools for a Morkie and their type and length of coat.

You will need a variety of brushes and combs to keep your Morkie's coat in good condition, that will include a soft bristle brush, a slicker brush and a pin brush.

As well as your collection of brushes, you will need to invest in a metal comb, a flea comb and perhaps a mat splitter.

9. Equipment & Supplies Required

A **bristle brush** with its clusters of tightly-packed bristles will remove loose hair, dirt and debris while gently stimulating the skin, improving circulation and adding shine to the coat.

A **pin brush** usually has an oval head with wire bristles that are individually spaced and embedded into a flexible rubber pad.

Most guardians prefer pin brushes with rubber tips as these help to prevent a wire from accidentally piercing a dog's sensitive skin.

A pin brush is more normally used following a thorough bristle brushing to lift and fluff the hair at the end of a grooming session.

A **slicker brush** has short, thin, wire bristles arranged closely together and anchored to a flat, often rectangular, surface that's attached to a handle.

A slicker brush is an ideal grooming tool for helping to remove mats and tangles from a Morkie's coat. Slicker brushes are often used as a finishing brush after the use of a pin brush to smooth the dog's coat and create a shiny finish.

Mat Splitters, as the name suggests, are tools for splitting apart matted hair, and they come in three different types, including the letter opener style, the safety razor style and the curved blade style.

All of these tools are used to split matted fur into smaller, lengthwise pieces, with minimal discomfort to the dog, so that you or your groomer can untangle or shave the area with a clipper.

Combs are very useful for getting down to the base of any tangles in a dog's coat and working them loose before they develop into painful mats.

Most metal combs have a combination of widely spaced and narrow spaced teeth and are designed so that if you run into a tangle, you can switch to the wider spaced teeth while you work it out, without pulling and irritating your dog.

NOTE: Some combs have rotating teeth which makes the process of removing tangles from your Morkie's coat much easier on them without the pain of pulling and snagging.

Flea combs, as the name suggests, are designed for the specific purpose of removing fleas from a dog's coat.

A flea comb is usually small in size for maneuvering in tight spaces, and may be made of plastic or metal with the teeth of the comb placed very close together, to trap hiding fleas.

As well, you will want to keep a good quality pair of small **scissors** in your Morkie grooming box, even if you do not want to do the full grooming process yourself, so that you can regularly trim around your Morkie's eyes between full grooming sessions.

If you are planning to groom your Morkie yourself, you will need to invest in good quality scissors of several lengths that can cost anywhere between $30 and $200 each (£18 and £119) or more.

10. Products

a) Shampoos

NEVER make the mistake of using human shampoo or conditioner for bathing your Morkie because dogs have a different pH balance than humans.

For example, shampoo for humans has a pH balance of 5.5, whereas shampoo formulated for our canine companions has an almost neutral pH balance of 7.5.

Any shampoo with a lower pH balance will be harmful to your dog because it will be too harshly acidic for their coat and skin, which can create skin problems.

Always purchase a shampoo for your dog that is specially formulated to be gentle and moisturizing on your Morkie's coat and skin, that will not strip the natural oils, and which will nourish your dog's coat to give it a healthy shine.

As a general rule, always read the instructions provided on the shampoo bottle, and avoid shampoos containing insecticides or harsh chemicals.

Tip: if your Morkie is suffering from an infestation of fleas, you may want to bathe them with shampoo containing pyrethrum (a botanical extract found in small, white daisies) or a shampoo containing citrus oil.

b) Conditioners

While many of us humans use a conditioner after we shampoo our own hair, a large number of us canine guardians forget to use a conditioner on our own dog's coat after bathing.

Even if the bathing process is one that you wish to complete as quickly as possible, you will want to reconsider this little oversight because, just as conditioning our human hair improves its condition, the same is true for our dog's coat.

Conditioning your Morkie's coat will not only make it look and feel better, conditioning will also add additional benefits, including:

- preventing the escape of natural oils and moisture;
- keeping the coat cleaner for a longer period of time;
- repairing a coat that has become damaged or dry;
- restoring a soft, silky feel;
- a conditioned coat will dry more quickly;
- protection from the heat of the dryer and breakage from tangles during toweling , combing or brushing;

Spend the extra two minutes to condition your Morkie's coat after bathing because the benefits of doing so will be appreciated by both you and your dog who will have an overall healthy coat and skin with a natural shine.

c) De-tanglers

There are many de-tangling products you can purchase which will make the job of combing and removing mats much easier on both you and your Morkie, especially if you have opted to let their hair grow longer.

De-tangling products work by making the hair slippery, and while some de-tanglers work well when used full strength, you may prefer a lighter, spray-in product.

As well, there are silicone products and grooming powders, or you can even use corn starch to effectively lubricate the hair to help with removing mats and tangles before bathing.

d) Styptic Powder

You will always want to avoid causing any pain when trimming your Morkie's toenails, because you don't want to destroy their trust in you regularly performing this task.

However, accidents do happen, therefore if you accidentally cut into the vein in the toenail, know that you will cause your dog pain, and the toenail will bleed.

Therefore, it is always a good idea to keep some styptic powder (often called "Kwik Stop") in your grooming kit. Dip a moistened finger into the powder and apply it immediately to the end of the bleeding nail.

The quickest way to stop a nail from bleeding is to immediately apply styptic powder and firm pressure for a few seconds.

Tip: if you do not have styptic powder or a styptic pencil available, there are several home remedies that can help stop the bleeding, including a mixture of baking soda and corn starch, or simply cornstarch alone. Also, a cold, wet teabag or rubbing with scent-free soap can also be effective. These home remedies will not be as instantly effective as styptic powder.

e) Ear Powders

Ear powders, which can be purchased at any pet store, are designed to help keep your dog's ears dry while at the same time inhibiting the growth of bacteria that can lead to infections.

f) Ear Cleaning Solutions

Your local pet store will offer a wide variety of ear cleaning creams, drops, oils, rinses, solutions and wipes specially formulated for cleaning your dog's ears.

As well, there are also many home remedies that will just as efficiently clean your dog's ears.

Note: because a dog's ears are a very sensitive area, always read the labels before purchasing products and avoid any solutions that list alcohol as the main ingredient.

g) Home Ear Cleaning Solutions

The following are three effective home solutions that will efficiently clean your dog's ears:

Witch Hazel is a natural anti-inflammatory that works well to cleanse and protect against infection while encouraging faster healing of minor skin traumas.

A 50:50 solution of **Organic Apple Cider Vinegar and Purified Water** has been used as an external folk medicine for decades. This mixture is a gentle and effective solution that kills germs while naturally healing.

A 50:50 solution of **Hydrogen Peroxide and Purified Water** is useful for cleansing wounds and dissolving ear wax.

Whatever product you decide to use for cleaning your dog's ears, always be careful about what you put into your dog's ears and thoroughly dry them after cleaning.

h) Canine Toothpastes

When it comes time to brush a dog's teeth, this is where many guardians fail miserably, using the excuse that *"my dog doesn't like it"*. Whether they like it or otherwise, is not the issue, because in order to keep your Morkie healthy, they must have healthy teeth and the only way to ensure this, is to brush their teeth every day.

The many canine toothpastes on the market are usually flavored with beef or chicken in an attempt to appeal to the dog's taste buds, while others may be infused with mint or some other breath freshening ingredient in an attempt to appeal to humans by improving the dog's breath.

Honestly, your dog is not going to be begging for you to brush his or her teeth no matter how tasty the paste might be, therefore, effectiveness, in the shortest period of time, will be more of a deciding factor than whether or not your dog prefers the taste of the toothpaste.

Some dog toothpastes contain baking soda, which is the same mild abrasive found in many human pastes, and is designed to gently scrub the teeth. However, just how much time you will have to spend scrubbing your dog's teeth, before they've had enough, may be too minimal to make these pastes very effective.

Other types of canine toothpastes are formulated with enzymes that are designed to work chemically by breaking down tartar or plaque in the dog's mouth. These pastes do not need to be washed off your dog's teeth and are safe for them to swallow. Whether or not they remain on the dog's teeth long enough to do any good might be debatable.

Tip: old-fashioned hydrogen peroxide cleans while killing germs and keeping teeth white. Just dip your dog's toothbrush in a capful of hydrogen peroxide, shake off the excess, and brush their teeth. There will such a small amount in your dog's mouth that you don't need to worry about them swallowing it.

i) Paw Creams

Depending upon the types of surfaces our canine counterparts usually walk on, they may suffer from cracked or rough pads.

You can restore resiliency and keep your Morkie's paws in healthy condition by regularly applying a cream or lotion to protect their paw pads.

TIP: a good time to do this is just after you have clipped their nails.

11. Professional Grooming

If you decide that you are not interesting in buying all the equipment (electric clippers, blades, scissors, nail clippers, combs, brushes, table, etc.) or enrolling yourself in a $4,000 (£2,388) course to learn how to professionally groom your Morkie yourself, you will want to locate a trusted professional service to do this for you.

The best way to find a groomer is to ask others who they use and whether they are happy with the results.

If you have decided to keep your Morkie clipped short in a puppy cut, you will need to take them for a full grooming session approximately every 6 to 8 weeks.

An average price for professionally grooming a small Morkie will usually start around $40 (£24) and could be considerably more depending upon whether the salon is also bathing and trimming nails.

Chapter 11: Daily Feeding and Care

1) Feeding Puppies

For growing puppies, a general feeding rule of thumb is to feed 10% of the puppy's present body weight or between 2% and 3% of their projected adult weight each day.

Keep in mind that high energy puppies will require extra protein to help them grow and develop into healthy adult dogs, especially during their first two years of life.

There are now many foods on the market that are formulated for all stages of a dog's life (including the puppy stage), so whether you choose one of these foods or a food specially formulated for puppies, they will need to be fed smaller meals more frequently throughout the day (3 or 4 times), until they are at least one year of age.

NOTE: choose quality sources of meat protein for healthy puppies and dogs, including beef, buffalo, chicken, duck, fish, hare, lamb, ostrich, pork, rabbit, turkey, venison, or any other source of wild meaty protein.

2) Feeding Adults

An adult dog will generally need to be fed 2 to 3% of their body weight each day. Read the labels and avoid foods that contain a high amount of grains and other fillers. Choose foods that list high quality meat protein as the main ingredient.

TIP: grated parmesan cheese sprinkled on a Morkie's dinner will help to stop picky eaters from ignoring their food.

3) Treats

Since the creation of the first dog treat over 150 years ago the myriad of choices available on every pet store, feed store and grocery store shelf almost outnumbers those looking forward to eating them.

Today's treats are not just for making us guilty humans feel better because it makes us happy to give our fur friends something they really like, today's treats are designed to improve our dog's health.

Some of us humans treat our dogs, just because, others use treats for training purposes, others for health, while still others treat for a combination of reasons.

Whatever reason you choose to give treats to your Morkie, keep in mind that if we treat our dogs too often throughout the day, we may create a picky eater who will no longer want to eat their regular meals.

As well, if the treats we are giving are high calorie, we may be putting our dog's health in jeopardy by allowing them to become overweight.

4) Treats to Avoid

a) Rawhide

Rawhide is soaked in an ash/lye solution to remove every particle of meat, fat and hair and then further soaked in bleach to remove remaining traces of the ash/lye solution. Now that the product is no longer food, it no longer has to comply with food regulations.

While the hide is still wet it is shaped into rawhide chews, and upon drying it shrinks to approximately 1/4 of its original size.

Further, arsenic based products are often used as preservatives, and antibiotics and insecticides are added to kill bacteria that also fight against good bacteria in your dog's intestines.

The collagen fibers in the rawhide make it very tough and long lasting which makes this chew a popular choice for humans to give to their dogs because it satisfies the dog's natural urge to chew while providing many hours of quiet entertainment.

Sadly, when a dog chews a rawhide treat, they ingest many harsh chemicals and when your dog swallows a piece of rawhide, that piece now can swell up to four times its size inside your dog's stomach, which can cause anything from mild to severe gastric blockages that could become life threatening and require surgery.

b) Pigs Ears

These treats are actually the ears of pigs, and while most dogs will eagerly devour them, they are extremely high in fat, which can cause stomach upsets, vomiting and diarrhea for many dogs.

Pigs ears are often processed and preserved with unhealthy chemicals that discerning dog guardians will not want to feed their dogs. While pig ears are generally not considered to be a healthy treat choice for any dog, they should be especially avoided for any dog who may be at risk of being overweight.

c) Hoof Treats

Many humans give cow, horse and pig hooves to their dogs as treats because they consider them to be *"natural"*.

The truth is that after processing these *"treats"* they retain little, if any, of their *"natural"* qualities.

Hoof treats are processed with preservatives, including insecticides, lead, bleach, arsenic based products, and antibiotics to kill bacteria, that can also harm the good bacteria in your dog's intestines, and if all bacteria is not killed in these meat based products before feeding them to your dog, they could also suffer from Salmonella poisoning.

Hooves can also cause chipping or breaking of your dog's teeth as well as perforation or blockages in your dog's intestines.

5) Healthy Treats

a) Hard Treats

There are so many choices of hard, or crunchy treats available that come in many varieties of shapes, sizes and flavors, that you may have a difficult time choosing. If your Morkie will eat them, hard treats will help to keep their teeth cleaner.

Whatever you do choose, read the labels and make sure that the ingredients are high quality and appropriately sized for your Morkie friend.

b) Soft Treats

Soft, chewy treats are also available in a wide variety of flavors, shapes and sizes for all the different needs of our fur friends and are often used for training purposes as they have a stronger smell.

Often smaller dogs, such as the Morkie, prefer the soft, chewy treats over the hard crunchy ones.

c) Dental Treats

Dental treats or chews are designed with the specific purpose of helping your Morkie to maintain healthy teeth and gums. They usually require intensive chewing and are often shaped with high ridges and bumps to exercise the jaw and massage gums while removing plaque build-up near the gum line.

d) Freeze-Dried and Jerky Treats

Freeze-dried and jerky treats offer a tasty morsel most dogs find irresistible as they are usually made of simple, meaty ingredients, such as liver, poultry and seafood. These treats are usually light weight and easy to carry around, which means they can also be great as training treats.

e) Human Food Treats

You will want to be very careful when feeding human foods to dogs as treats, because many of our foods contain additives and ingredients that could be toxic and harmful.

Be certain to choose simple, fresh foods with minimal or no processing, such as lean meat, poultry or seafood, and even if your Morkie will eat anything put in front of them, be aware that many common human foods, such as grapes, raisins, onions and chocolate are poisonous to dogs.

f) Training Treats

While any sort of treat can be used as an extra incentive during training sessions, soft treats are often used for training purposes because of their stronger smell and smaller sizes.

Yes, we humans love to treat our dogs, whether for helping to teach the new puppy to go pee outside, teaching the adolescent dog new commands, for trick training, for general good behavior, or for no reason at all, other than that they just gave us the *"look"*.

Make sure the treats you choose are high quality, so that you can help to keep your Morkie both happy and healthy, and generally, the treats you feed should not make up more than approximately 10% of their daily food intake.

6) Choosing the Right Food

In order to choose the right food for your Morkie, first, it's important to understand the canine physiology and what Mother Nature intended when she created our furry friends.

More than 230 years ago, in 1785, the English *Sportman's dictionary* described the best diet for a dog's health in an article entitled "Dog", describing the best food for dog to be something called *"Greaves"*, described as *"the sediment of melted tallow. It is made into cakes for dogs' food. In Scotland and parts of the US it is called cracklings."*

From the meagre beginning of the first commercially made dog food has sprung a massively lucrative and vastly confusing industry that has only recently begun to evolve beyond those early days of feeding our dogs the dregs of human leftovers because it was cheap and convenient for us.

Even today, the majority of dog food choices have far more to do with being convenient for us humans to serve than it does with being a diet truly designed to be a well-balanced, healthy food choice for a canine.

The dog food industry is big business and as such, because there are now almost limitless choices, there is much confusion and endless debate when it comes to answering the question, *"What is the best food for my dog?"*

Educating yourself by talking to experts and reading everything you can find on the subject, plus taking into consideration several relevant factors, will help to answer the dog food question.

For instance, where you live may dictate what sorts of foods you have access to. Other factors to consider will include the particular requirements of your dog, such as their age, energy and activity levels.

Next will be expense, time and quality. While we all want to give our dogs the best food possible, many humans lead very busy lives and cannot, for instance, prepare their own dog food, but still want to feed a high quality diet that fits within their budget.

However, perhaps most important when choosing an appropriate diet for our dogs, is learning to be more observant of Mother Nature's design and taking a closer look at our dog's teeth, jaws and digestive tract.

While humans are herbivores who derive energy from eating plants, our canine companions are carnivores, which means they derive their energy and nutrient requirements from eating a diet consisting mainly or exclusively of flesh or animal tissues (ie. meat).

a) The Canine Teeth

The first part of your dog you will want to take a good look at when considering what to feed them, will be their teeth.

Unlike humans, who are equipped with wide, flat molars for grinding grains, vegetables and other plant-based materials, canine teeth are all pointed because they are designed to rip, shred and tear into animal meat and bone.

b) The Canine Jaw

Another obvious consideration when choosing an appropriate food source for our fur friends, is the fact that every canine is born equipped with powerful jaws and neck muscles for the specific purpose of being able to pull down and tear apart their hunted prey.

The structure of the jaw of every canine is such that it opens widely to hold large pieces of meat and bone, while the mechanics of a dog's jaw permits only vertical (up and down) movement that is designed for crushing.

c) The Canine Digestive Tract

A dog's digestive tract is short and simple and designed to move their natural choice of food (hide, meat and bone) quickly through their systems.

Vegetables and plant matter require more time to break down in the gastrointestinal tract, which in turn, requires a more complex digestive system than the canine body is equipped with.

The canine digestive system is simply unable to break down vegetable matter, which is why whole vegetables look pretty much the same going into your dog as they do coming out the other end.

Given the choice, most dogs would never choose to eat plants or vegetables and fruits over meat, however, we humans continue to feed them a kibble based diet that contains high amounts of vegetables and grains and low amounts of meat.

Plus, in order to get our dogs to eat fruits, vegetables and grains we usually have to flavor the food with meat or meat by-products.

How much healthier and long lived might our beloved fur friends be if, instead of largely ignoring nature's design for our canine companions, we chose to feed them whole, unprocessed, species-appropriate food?

With many hundreds of dog food brands to choose from, it's no wonder we humans are confused about what to feed our dogs to help them live long and healthy lives.

Following are some suggestions and questions that may help you choose a dog food company that you can feel comfortable with:

- how long they have been in business?
- is dog food their main industry?
- are they dedicated to their brand?
- are they easily accessible?
- if you contact them, do they honestly answer your questions?
- research the Company's Safety Standard
- look for pet food companies that set higher standards
- read the ingredients - where did they come from?
- are the ingredients something you would eat?
- are the ingredients farmed locally?
- was it cooked in a kitchen using standards you would trust?

- is the company certified under human food or organic guidelines?

Whatever you decide to feed your Morkie, keep in mind that, just as too much wheat, other grains and other fillers in our human diet is having detrimental effects on our health, the same can be very true for our best fur friends.

Our dogs are also suffering from many of the same life threatening diseases that are rampant in our human society as a direct result of consuming a diet high in genetically altered, impure, processed and packaged foods.

7) The Raw Diet

While some of us believe we are killing ourselves as well as our dogs with processed foods, others believe that there are dangers in feeding raw foods.

Those who are raw feeding advocates believe that the ideal diet for their dog is one which would be very similar to what a dog living in the wild would have access to, and these canine guardians are often opposed to feeding their dog any sort of commercially manufactured pet foods, because they consider them to be poor substitutes.

On the other hand, those opposed to feeding their dogs a raw or biologically appropriate raw food diet, believe that the risks associated with food-borne illnesses during the handling and feeding of raw meats outweigh the purported benefits.

Interestingly, even though the United States Food and Drug Administration (FDA) states that they do not advocate a raw diet for dogs, they do advise that for those who wish to take this route, following basic hygiene guidelines for handling raw meat can minimize any associated risks.

Further, high pressure pasteurization (HPP), which is high pressure, water based technology for killing bacterial, is USDA-approved for use on organic and natural food products, and is being utilized by many commercial raw pet food manufacturers.

Raw meats purchased at your local grocery store contain a much higher level of acceptable bacteria than raw food produced for dogs, because the meat purchased for human consumption is meant to be cooked, which will kill any bacteria that might be present.

This means that canine guardians feeding their dogs a raw food diet can be quite certain that commercially prepared raw foods sold in pet stores will be safer than raw meats purchased in grocery stores.

Many guardians of high energy, working breed dogs will agree that their dogs thrive on a raw or BARF (Biologically Appropriate Raw Food) diet and strongly believe that the potential benefits of feeding a raw dog food diet are many, including:

- healthy, shiny coats
- decreased shedding
- fewer allergy problems
- healthier skin
- cleaner teeth
- fresher breath
- higher energy levels
- improved digestion
- smaller stools

- strengthened immune system
- increased mobility in arthritic pets
- general increase or improvement in overall health

All dogs, whether working breed or lap dogs are amazing athletes in their own right, therefore every dog deserves to be fed the best food available.

A raw diet is a direct evolution of what dogs ate before they became our domesticated pets and we turned toward commercially prepared, easy to serve dry dog food that required no special storage or preparation.

The BARF diet is all about feeding our dogs what they are designed to eat by returning them to their evolutionary diet.

When considering the health of your Morkie, it is certainly worth remembering that just as too much wheat and processed foods in our human diet is having detrimental effects on our health, the same can be very true for our best fur friends who are also suffering from many of the same life threatening diseases that are rampant in our society today.

8) The Dehydrated Diet

Dehydrated dog food comes in both raw and cooked forms and these foods are usually air dried to reduce moisture to the level where bacterial growths are inhibited.

The appearance of de-hydrated dog food is very similar to dry kibble and the typical feeding methods include adding warm water before serving, which makes this type of diet both healthy for our dogs and convenient for us to serve.

Dehydrated recipes are made from minimally processed fresh whole foods to create a healthy and nutritionally balanced meal that will meet or exceed the dietary requirements for healthy canines.

Dehydrating removes only the moisture from the fresh ingredients, which usually means that because the food has not already been cooked at a high temperature, more of the overall nutrition is retained.

A de-hydrated diet is a convenient way to feed your dog a nutritious diet because all you have to do is add warm water, and wait five minutes while the food re-hydrates so your Morkie can enjoy a warm meal.

9) The Kibble Diet

While many canine guardians are starting to take a closer look at the food choices they are making for their furry companions, there is no mistaking that the convenience and relative economy of dry dog food kibble, that had its beginnings in the 1940's, continues to be the most popular pet food choice for most dog friendly humans.

Some 75 years later, the massive pet food industry offers up a confusingly large number of choices with hundreds of different manufacturers and brand names lining the shelves of veterinarian offices, grocery stores and pet food aisles.

While feeding a high quality bagged kibble diet that has been flavored to appeal to dogs and supplemented with vegetables and fruits to appeal to humans, may keep most every Morkie companion happy and healthy, you will need to decide whether this is the best diet for them.

10) The Right Bowl

Following is a brief description of the different categories and types of dog bowls that would be appropriate choices for your Morkie's particular needs.

Automatic Watering Bowls: are standard dog bowls (often made out of plastic) that are attached to a reservoir container, which is designed to keep water constantly available to your dog as long as there is water remaining in the storage compartment.

Ceramic/Stoneware Bowls: are a great choice for those who like options in personality, color and shape.

Elevated Bowls: raised dining table dog bowls are a tidy and classy choice that will make your dog's dinner time a more comfortable experience while getting the bowls off the floor.

No Skid Bowls: are for dogs who push their bowls across the floor when eating. A non-skid dog bowl will help keep the feed bowl where you put it.

No Tip Bowls: are designed to prevent the messy type of doggy eater from flipping over their dinner or water bowls.

Stainless Steel Bowls: are as close to indestructible as a bowl can be, plus they are sanitary and easy to clean and water stays cooler for a longer period of time in a stainless bowl.

Wooden Bowls: for those humans concerned about stylish home decor, wooden dog bowl dining stations are beautiful pieces of furniture unto themselves that can enhance your home decor.

Travel Bowls: are a convenient, practical and handy addition to the traveling canine. Instead of a cloth bowl that is difficult to clean, consider a space saving, collapsible dog bowl, made out of hygienic, renewable bamboo that comes in fun colors and different sizes, making it perfect for every travel bowl needs.

If you would like to learn more about all the many dog bowl choices available, visit DogBowlForYourDog.com, which is a comprehensive, one-stop website dedicated to explaining the ins and outs of every food bowl imaginable and helping you find the perfect bowl for all your Morkie's needs.

11) Exercise

Every dog is an athlete and therefore they need daily exercise to say fit and healthy. The energetic Morkie is no exception to this rule. Every Morkie will love going for walks with their guardian several times every day.

As well, taking your Morkie for a disciplined walk, where they are on leash and walking beside you without straining on the leash or trying to lead you, will reinforce that you are the boss and they are the follower.

Any type of disciplined exercise you can do with your Morkie will help to exercise both their body and their mind and will burn off daily energy reserves so that your Morkie will be a happy and contented lap dog.

If you find that your Morkie is being a pest by chewing inappropriate items around the home or being demanding of your time, or especially unruly when visitors come to call, this is likely because they are not being exercised often enough, or long enough to drain out their daily pent up energy.

A healthy, adult Morkie will thrive when being walked several times each day and will enjoy the challenge of being engaged in other forms of disciplined activity, such as Agility.

12) Playtime

Every dog needs some regular play time each day, and the Morkie is no exception to this general care rule because this is a loving, energetic companion.

While every Morkie will be different with respect to what types of games they may enjoy, most Morkie's will enjoy a game of ball or a gentle tug-o-war with a soft rope. While some Morkie's might be great a playing fetch, others may like to chase after a ball or stick, but may have little interest in actually bringing it back to you.

Perhaps a fun game of *"Search"*, where you ask your Morkie to "Sit/Stay" while you hide a favorite treat that they then have to find, will appeal to the Morkie's ancient hunting instincts.

After a disciplined walk with your Morkie, they will also enjoy being given the opportunity for some off leash freedom to run, play and socialize with other like-sized dogs.

13) Daily Grooming

Daily grooming is a must for any Morkie. Get into the routine of spending at least 15 minutes each day brushing or combing your Morkie, trimming the hair away from their eyes, checking their nails and brushing their teeth.

14) Safe Traveling

Far too many canine guardians do nothing to protect their companions when traveling with them in their vehicles.

According to a 2011 American Automobile Association study, only about 16% of dog owners restrain their pets when riding in a vehicle, and of those who are trying, many are not properly securing their beloved pets.

That leaves 84% of people who let their dogs roam freely about the inside of their vehicles, leaving them at serious risk of being injured or killed in an automobile accident.

When traveling at only 30 miles per hour (48.28 km/h) when involved in an accident, a small, ten pound (4.54 kg), unrestrained dog will be subjected to approximately 300 pounds (136 kilogram) of force, which is certainly enough to seriously injure or kill a Morkie.

There is no denying that dogs that are not properly restrained become projectiles in any sort of vehicle crash.

As well, many drivers permit their small dogs to sit on their lap when driving, which is not only distracting to the driver, but if involved in an accident, the vehicle's airbags will deploy at 300 mph (482.8 km/h) which can easily snap the neck of a small dog.

a) Faulty Restraints

Many dog lovers may be laboring under the misconception that they are doing the right thing by buckling their canine companions into a safety harness because they are unaware that many of these dog harnesses that are supposed to keep furry passengers safe have a 100% failure rate.

Statistics collected by the Center for Pet Safety (CPS) have shown that every popular restraint tested with dog dummies, traveling at a sedate 30 mph (48.28 km/h), not only failed, but also indicated that serious injuries or deaths were highly likely.

Most restraints that were tested in the CPS study allowed dogs to easily become flying projectiles during vehicle accidents because the harnesses were simply not strong enough to keep them in their seats, and in many cases the restraints could actually choke the dog during a crash.

When the MGA Research Corporation carried out a pilot study for The Center for Pet Safety (CPS), in which they tested 12 major brands of pet harnesses, the results indicated a 100% failure rate.

According to the American Kennel Club, these safety harness tests were carried out using the average weights of the ten most popular breeds of dogs, including the Labrador Retriever, the German Shepherd, the Golden Retriever, the Beagle, the Bulldog, the Yorkshire Terrier, the Boxer, the Poodle, the Rottweiler and the Dachshund.

The founder and chairman of CPS, believes that, "*Saying that these products prevent your pet from becoming a projectile in an accident is a potentially misleading statement.*"

Law enforcement agencies, safety advocates, insurance companies, and concerned dog owners need to keep pressing for the development of a standard for dog safety equipment, to insist that all such equipment pass a government regulated crash test before being sold as safe for travel.

The safest travel arrangement for any dog is to secure them inside a travel bag or kennel, followed by finding a safety restraint that is crash and strength tested and certified to be safe for your dog.

b) Kennels

If you opt to contain your best friend inside a kennel, crate or travel bag, you absolutely must make sure that the kennel or bag is very securely attached with the vehicle's seatbelt or even better, with special tie downs that are bolted to the floor of the vehicle.

A small dog kennel or crate will easily fit on the back seat of most vehicles and can be secured with the vehicle's restraint system. A Morkie riding inside a kennel, crate or travel bag inside your vehicle will have the best protection in the case of a rollover accident.

There is at least one manufacturer of a travel bag restraint system, called 'Sleepypod™", designed for pets up to 15 pounds (6.8 kg) that goes the extra mile for safety and actually puts its own products through the child safety seat test. All four models of the Sleepypod™ have passed the 30 mph (48.28 km/h) crash test.

c) Harness Restraints

The Kurgo Tru-Fit Smart harness has been crash and strength tested and with its steel nesting buckles has a tensile strength tested to withstand a force of 2250 pounds (1120 kilogram). The crash test videos of this product depict a 35 pound (15.9 kg) dummy dog traveling at 30 miles per hour (48.28 km/h), recorded at an accredited University test facility.

The Ruff Rider Roadie® harness successfully passed the preliminary test criteria for both dynamic and static load limits.

Ruff Rider's only product is the Roadie® travel restraint which was invented by dog owner, Carl Goldberg, after his pet was ejected through the front windshield in a minor collision.

The design of the Roadie® is so unique it was awarded three (3) patents. Over the past 20 years Roadie® has helped protect many dogs during vehicle accidents.

Sleepypod™ manufactures a safety harness called *"Clickit Utility"* that is the first dog safety harness to incorporate three-points of attachment to absorb force in a frontal collision by dissipating energy and keeping the dog in the car seat during an impact (patents pending). Clickit Utility can also be used in the cargo area and includes a d-ring on the back of the vest so it can be used as a walking harness.

Keep your Morkie safe when traveling in your vehicle. Do your research and either transport your dog inside a kennel, or find a safety harness that is strength tested and certified to be able to keep your Morkie safe in the event of an accident.

d) Sherpa for Small Dogs

 The Sherpa is a name that refers to a soft-sided dog carrier with zippered pockets for carrying important papers, treats, baggies, etc., that has mesh sides for superior ventilation.

While there is an actual "Sherpa" brand name, this name has become synonymous with any type of soft sided carrier bag.

The bag has handles as well as a shoulder strap and some even have wheels, so your Morkie puppy or dog will be able to safely travel anywhere in style and comfort.

A Morkie puppy will remain small when fully grown, therefore they are the perfect candidate for learning to travel about inside a Sherpa or soft-sided travel bag, such as the Sleepypod™.

When they are young puppies, get them used to Sherpa travel by putting them inside their bag every time they need to go outside, and before you bring them back inside. When you do this, a Morkie puppy will very quickly learn to love scooting into their bag because they associate it with the fun activity of going outside with you.

Once your Morkie puppy becomes used to Sherpa travel, it will be very easy for them to travel with you wherever you go, including public transportation (buses), boats, planes and vehicles, and the best way to start them getting used to this idea is as soon as you bring your new puppy home.

"Sleepypod™" manufactures various styles of high end travel bags for small dogs, such as the Morkie, and puts their bags through rigorous crash testing to ensure they are totally safe.

Although these bags are considerably more costly than many other canine travel bags or Sherpas, you will have peace of mind knowing that your little Morkie will always be safe when riding inside one.

e) Air Travel

A small dog, like the Morkie, can be *"carry on baggage"* if the carrier fits the airline regulations, which state that a pet carrier must be able to fit under the seat in front of you. Most soft carriers are airline approved and under seat dimensions are generally as follows:

Window Seat: 19" L x 14" W x 8.25" H
[48.26 cm L x 35.56 cm W x 20.955 cm H]
Middle Seat: 19" L x 19" W x 8.25" H
[48.26 cm L x 48.26 cm W x 20.955 cm H]
Aisle Seat: 19" L x 14" W x 8.25" H
[48.26 cm L x 35.56 cm W x 20.955 cm H]

For in-cabin travel by plane, your pet must be able to stand up and turn around comfortably in the bag. Airlines also require an absorbent liner in the bag, which could be a pee pad, an old towel, a favorite blanket, or a cozy, faux lambskin liner.

Many styles of canine carrier bags are officially approved for airline travel, and when you make your flight reservations, don't forget to reserve for your Morkie as well, because there is generally a small charge for in-cabin travel.

Chapter 12: Socializing

1. With Other Dogs and Pets

Generally speaking, the majority of an adult dog's habits and behavioral traits will be formed between the ages of birth and one year of age. This is why it will be very important to introduce your Morkie puppy to a wide variety and types of locations, sights, sounds and smells during this formative period in their young life.

Your Morkie puppy will learn how to behave, in all these various circumstances, by following your lead, feeling your energy and watching how you react in every situation.

For instance, never accidentally reward your Morkie puppy for displaying fear or growling at another dog or person by picking them up.

Picking up a Morkie puppy or dog at this time, when they are displaying unbalanced energy, actually turns out to be a reward for them, and you will be teaching them to continue with this type of behavior.

As well, picking up a puppy literally places them in a top dog position, where they are higher and more dominant than the person or dog they just growled at.

The correct action to take in such a situation is to gently correct your Morkie puppy, with a firm, yet calm energy by distracting them with a "no", so that they learn to let you deal with the situation on their behalf. If you allow a fearful puppy to deal with situations that unnerve them all by themselves, they may learn to react with fear or aggression to unfamiliar circumstances and you will have created a problem that could escalate into something quite serious as they grow older.

The same is true of situations where a young puppy may feel the need to protect themselves from a bigger or older dog that may come charging in for a sniff.

It is the guardian's responsibility to protect the puppy so that they do not think they must react with fear or aggression to protect themselves.

Once your Morkie puppy has received all their vaccinations, you can take them out to public dog parks and various locations where many dogs are found.

Before allowing them to interact with other dogs or puppies, take them for a disciplined walk on leash so that they will be a little tired and less likely to immediately pounce on all other dogs.

Keep your puppy on leash and close beside you, because most puppies are a bundle of out of control energy, and you need to protect them while teaching them how far they can go before getting themselves into trouble with adult dogs who may not appreciate their excited playfulness.

Keep a close watch on your Morkie puppy to make sure they are not being overwhelmed by too many other dogs, or getting overly excited and stressed because it is your job to protect your puppy. If your puppy shows any signs of aggression or domination toward another puppy, dog or person, you must immediately step in and calmly discipline them, otherwise by doing nothing, you will be allowing them to get into situations that could become serious behavioral issues as they grow in age and size.

No matter the age or size of your puppy, allowing them to display aggression or domination over another dog or person is never a laughing matter and this type of behavior must be immediately curtailed.

2. With Other People

Take your puppy everywhere with you and introduce them to many different people of all ages, sizes and ethnicities. Most people will automatically be drawn to you when they see you have a puppy because few humans can resist a cute puppy.

Most people will come to you and want to interact with your puppy and if they ask if they can hold your puppy, this is also a good way to socialize your puppy and show them that humans are friendly.

Do not let others (especially children) play roughly with your puppy or squeal at them in a high pitched voices because this can be very frightening for a young puppy. As well, you do not want to teach your puppy that humans are a source of excitement.

Be especially careful when introducing your puppy to young children who may accidentally hurt your puppy, because you don't want them to become fearful of children as this could lead to aggression later on in life.

Explain to children that your Morkie puppy is very young and that they must be calm and gentle when playing or interacting in any way.

3. Within Different Environments

It can be a big mistake not to take the time to introduce your Morkie puppy to a wide variety of different environments because when they are not comfortable with different sights and sounds, this could cause them possible trauma later in their adult life.

Be creative and take your puppy everywhere you can imagine when they are young so that no matter where they travel, whether strolling a busy city sidewalk or along a deserted seashore, they will be comfortable.

Don't make the mistake of only taking your Morkie puppy into areas where you live and will always travel because they need to also be comfortable visiting areas you might not often visit, such as noisy construction sites or airports.

Your puppy needs to see all sorts of sights, sounds and situations so that they will not become fearful should they need to travel with you to any of these areas.

Your Morkie puppy will take its cues from you, which means that when you are calm and in control of every situation, they will learn to be the same.

For instance, put your puppy in their Sherpa bag and take them to the airport where they can watch people and hear planes landing and taking off, take them to a local park where they can see a baseball game, or take them to the local zoo or farm and let them get a close up look at horses, pigs and ducks.

When you take your Morkie puppy everywhere you will be teaching them to be a calm and well balanced member of your family in every situation.

A good idea is to introduce your dog to new sounds by playing music of those sounds e.g. in a car or in the house and pretend everything is perfectly normal when the sounds are being played. If you do this when the dog is still very young, it is likely he won't care about "strange" noises.

A few examples of noises you could get your dog used to: airplanes, firework, the sound of a hoover, hot air balloon, crying children, a meowing cat, kids playing in the park, cars driving on the road, car hooters, a bicycle bell, thunder, etc.

There are CD's available online with all these sort of sounds recorded on for you to play in the presence of your dog. Just search for it online.

Chapter 13: Morkie Vital Statistics

1. Country of Origin

While some agree that the *"toy"* sized Morkie hybrid originated in the US, there are others who will argue that this little dog originated in Canada, more precisely in Quebec.

2. Litter Size

On average, 3 to 5 puppies

3. Height and Weight

The Morkie generally weighs between 4 and 10 pounds (1.8 to 3.6 kilos) with an average weight between 5 and 7 pounds (2.26 and 3.17 kilos) and stands between 6 and 8 inches (15.24 to 20.32 centimeters) when measured at the withers (top of the shoulder).

4. Temperature & Heart Rate

Temperature: 100.5 to 102.5 degrees Fahrenheit (38.05 to 39.16 Celsius).

Respiratory Rate: 10 to 20 per minute

Pulse: Puppies, 120 to 160 per minute. Adults, 60 to 140 per minute.

Gums: should be pink

5. Lifespan

While they may live longer, on average, the Morkie lifespan will be between 10 and 13 years.

6. Intelligence

Stanley Coren, a professor of psychology at the University of British Columbia, in Vancouver, B.C., Canada, published *The Intelligence of Dogs* in 1994. Since then this book has become the standard for rating the particular intelligence of different canine breeds.

Coren's book describes three categories of dog intelligence:

(1) *instinctive intelligence;*

(2) *adaptive intelligence,* and

(3) *working and obedience intelligence.*

Instinctive intelligence refers to a dog's ability to carry out tasks it was bred to perform, such as guarding, herding, hunting, pointing, retrieving, or supplying companionship.

Adaptive intelligence refers to how well a dog is able to solve problems on its own.

Working and obedience intelligence refers to how quickly a dog is able to learn from humans.

The Maltese dog holds the 59th position in the *"Fair Working/Obedience Intelligence"* category and the Yorkshire Terrier breed ranks 27 out of a possible 79 in the *"Above*

Average Working Dog" category, which means that the pairing of these two purebreds, depending upon which breed's genes are more dominant, could mean that the Morkie will take on the *"above average"* genes of the Yorkshire Terrier, or the *"fair"* intelligence of the Maltese.

In other words, if one is to agree with the findings of Stanley Coren, on the Yorkshire Terrier side of this hybrid, the Morkie can understand new commands after 15 to 25 repetitions and obey first commands approximately 70% of the time, or on the Maltese side of the hybrid, the Morkie may only understand new commands after 40 to 80 repetitions, and may obey first commands approximately 30% of the time.

7. Hybrid Vigor

Remember those stories you used to hear when you were a kid when people talked about dogs and how a *"mutt"* was the best kind?

What you may have heard about mutts being healthier and making better pets is not an old wive's tail, but actually true.

The term *"hybrid vigor"* is a real phenomenon that occurs in every animal (& plant) species during the first pairing or when two separate species are bred together.

Therefore, although all Morkies will not be a first generation cross between a Maltese and a Yorkshire Terrier, those who are, will be healthier and mentally more stable that either of the litter's purebred parents.

When both parents share the same traits, in a purebred line, the offspring they produce will be much more likely to display a disease or health problem common to the breed.

On the other hand, while puppies resulting from breeding two distinctly different purebred canines will usually retain physical attributes common to both parents, the puppies will display characteristics which lie somewhere between the two parents.

With respect to health issues, if only one purebred parent carries a trait or health problem common to the breed, when breeding these two purebreds together, this gene will be recessive in the puppies.

Hybrid vigor will be lost every time a Morkie is bred to another Morkie because there will be more genes that the Morkie will share in common.

Breeding a Morkie to a Morkie can also result in generations of puppies that are more prone to health issues.

8. Living Conditions

The Morkie, because of their small size does not require an expansive living environment in order to be happy. This small breed will be perfectly fine living in an apartment or condominium complex.

However, they can be energetic little dogs that need daily exercise outside of the home. A full grown Morkie will need to burn off their daily pent up energy by going for at least two good walks of 30 minutes to an hour beside their human companions every day.

In order for this intelligent and social little dog to be happy and well balanced they will want to be close to their human family which means taking your Morkie everywhere with you, rather than leaving them alone for many hours in the day.

Chapter 14: Training

1. Trainability

As the Yorkshire Terrier has an above average intelligence and the Maltese is rated as having a fair intelligence, when pairing these two together your Morkie could be very bright and eager to learn or a little more on the stubborn side.

Generally speaking, the Morkie cross breed will be moderately easy to train so long as their guardian is gentle and patient, because using harsh or loud training methods could frighten a Morkie and cause them to shut down.

All training sessions should be happy and fun filled with plenty of rewards and positive reinforcement, which will ensure that your Morkie is an excellent student who looks forward to learning new commands and tricks.

2. Puppy Training

Most humans believe that they need to take their puppy to puppy classes, and generally speaking, this is a good idea for any young Morkie (after they have had their vaccinations), because it will help to get them socialized.

Beyond puppy classes for socializations reasons, hiring a professional dog whisperer for personalized private sessions to train the humans will be far more valuable than training situations where there are multiple dogs and humans together in one class as this can be very distracting for everyone concerned.

a) Three Most Important Words

"Come", **"Sit"** and **"Stay"** will be the three most important words you will ever teach your Morkie puppy.

These three basic commands will ensure that your Morkie remains safe in almost every circumstance.

For instance, when your puppy correctly learns the "Come" command, you can always quickly bring them back to your side should danger be approaching.

When you teach your Morkie puppy the "Sit" and "Stay" commands you will be further establishing your leadership role. A puppy that understands that their human guardian is their leader will be a safe and happy follower.

b) Choosing a Discipline Sound

Choosing a *"discipline sound"* that will be the same for every human family member will make it much easier for your puppy to learn what they can or cannot do and will be very useful when warning your puppy before they engage in unwanted behavior.

The best types of sounds are short and sharp so that you and your family members can quickly say them and so that the sound will immediately get the attention of your Morkie puppy to interrupt them when they are about to make a mistake.

It doesn't really matter what the sound is, so long as everyone in the family is consistent. A sound that is very effective for most puppies and dogs is a simple "UH" sound said sharply and with emphasis.

Most puppies and dogs respond immediately to this sound and if caught in the middle of doing something they are not supposed to be doing will quickly stop and give you their attention or back away from what they were doing.

3. Beginner Leash Lesson

Equipment: 4 or 6 foot leash, Martingale training collar.

The most important bonding exercise you will experience with your new Morkie puppy is when you go out for your daily walks together.

Far, far too many people ignore this critical time that is not only important for your puppy's exercise, it also helps to fulfill their natural roaming urges, while also being a time for them to learn discipline, when they learn to follow, trust and respect you as their guardian and leader.

As soon as you bring your new puppy home you will want to teach them how to walk at your side while on leash. Every time your puppy needs to go out to relieve themselves, slip on their collar and snap on that leash.

At first your Morkie puppy may struggle or fight against having a collar around their neck, because the sensation will be new to them. However, at the same time they will want to go with you, so exercise patience and encourage them to walk with you.

Be careful never to drag them, and if they pull backward and refuse to walk forward with you, simply stop for a moment, while keeping slight forward tension on the leash, until your Morkie puppy gives up and moves forward. Immediately reward them with your happy praise, and if they have a favorite treat, this can be an added incentive when teaching them to walk on their leash.

Always walk your puppy on your left side with the leash slack so that they learn that walking with you is a relaxing experience. Keep the leash short enough so that they do not have enough slack to get in front of you.

If they begin to create tension in the leash by pulling forward or to the side, simply stop moving, get them back beside you, and start over.

Be patient and consistent with your puppy and very soon they will understand exactly where their walking position is and will walk easily beside you without any pulling or leash tension.

Remember that walking with a new puppy is an exciting experience for them as they will want to sniff everything and explore their new world, so give them lots of understanding and don't expect them to be perfect all the time.

4. Surviving Adolescence

The adolescent period in a young Morkie's life, between the ages of 6 and 12 months, is the transitional stage of both physical and psychological development when they are physically almost full grown in size, yet their minds are still developing and they are testing their boundaries and the limits that their human counterparts will endure.

This can be a dangerous time in a puppy's life because this is when they start to make decisions on their own which can lead to developing unwanted behaviors.

Learning how to make decisions on their own would be perfectly normal and desirable if your Morkie puppy was living in the wild, amongst a pack of dogs, because it would be necessary for their survival.

However, when living within a human environment, your puppy must always adhere to human rules and it will be up to their human guardians to continue their vigilant, watchful guidance in order to make sure that they do.

Many humans are lulled into a false sense of security when their new Morkie puppy reaches the age of approximately six months, because the puppy has been well socialized, they have been to puppy classes and long since been house trained.

The real truth is that the serious work is only now beginning and the humans and their new Morkie puppy could be in for a time of testing that could seriously challenge the relationship and leave the humans wondering if they made the right decision to share their home with a Morkie.

If the human side of the relationship is not prepared for this transitional time in their young Morkie's life, their patience may be seriously tried, and the relationship of trust and respect that has been previously built can be damaged, sometimes irreparably.

While not all adolescent puppies will experience a noticeable adolescent period of craziness, because every puppy is different, most young dogs do commonly exhibit at least some of the usual adolescent behaviors, including reverting to previous puppy behaviors.

Some of these adolescent behaviors might include destructive chewing of objects they have previously shown no interest in, selective hearing or ignoring previously learned commands, displaying aggressive behavior, jumping on everyone, barking at everything that moves, or reverting to relieving themselves in the house, even though they were house trained months ago.

Keeping your cool and recognizing these adolescent signs is the first step toward helping to make this transition period easier on your Morkie puppy and all family members.

The first step to take that can help keep raging hormones at bay, is to spay or neuter your Morkie puppy just prior to the onset of adolescence, at around five or six months of age.

While spaying or neutering a Morkie puppy will not eliminate the adolescent phase, it will certainly help and at the same time will spare your puppy the added strain of both the physical and emotional changes that occur during sexual maturity.

As well, some female puppies will become extremely aggressive toward other dogs during a heat, and non-neutered males may become territorially aggressive and pick fights with other males.

Once your Morkie puppy has been spayed or neutered, you will want to become more active with your young dog, both mentally and physically by providing them with continued and more complex disciplined exercises.

This can be accomplished by enrolling your adolescent Morkie in dog whispering or more advanced training class, which will help them to continue their socialization skills while also developing their brain.

Even though it may be more difficult to train during this period, having the assistance of a professional and continuing the experience of ongoing socialization amongst other dogs of a similar size can be invaluable, as this is the time when many young dogs begin to show signs of antisocial behavior with other dogs as well as unknown humans.

When your Morkie is provided with sufficient daily exercise and continued socialization that provides interest and expands their mind, they will be able to transition through the adolescent stage of their life much more seamlessly.

5. Releasing Energy

The adolescent period in a puppy's life is a time of boundless energy and you will need to find ways to safely allow them to release this energy every day.

Since most humans cannot walk nearly fast enough to accommodate the needs of an energetic puppy, you will need to first walk your Morkie beside you on leash, and then find a safe place where they can run off leash, either chasing a ball or playing and running in an enclosed area with other similar sized dogs where you can always supervise.

6. The Unruly Adolescent

If your Morkie puppy happens to be especially unruly during their adolescent phase, you will need to simply limit their opportunities for making mistakes.

For instance, a puppy who is digging up the yard, or chewing up just about anything they can get their teeth on will need to be closely supervised so that you can direct their energy into less harmful areas.

It does absolutely no good to yell at your Morkie puppy for engaging in behavior you are not happy with, and in fact, yelling will only desensitize your young dog from listening to any of your commands.

Further, although you may eventually get the results you want, if you yell loud enough, your puppy will then be reacting out of fear, rather than respect, and this is not the type of relationship you want to have.

Displaying calm, yet assertive energy is the ONLY energy that works well to help your adolescent puppy understand what is required of them. All other humans emotions are "read" by puppies and dogs as being unstable, and not only will they not understand you, they will not respect you for displaying these types of energies.

An extremely rambunctious adolescent Morkie will need to have their free run privileges curtailed so that they are confined to areas where you can easily supervise them.

Make sure they are within eyesight at all times, so that if they do find an opportunity to make a mistake, you can quickly show them what is permitted and what is not.

Adolescence may also be a time when you might have to insist that your young Morkie sleeps in their crate with the door closed whenever you cannot supervise or when it's bedtime so they continue to understand that you have firm rules.

As well, keeping on top of house training is also a good idea during the adolescent period of your puppy's life because some adolescent puppies may forget that they are already house trained.

This means actually taking the time to be involved in the process by leashing up your Morkie and physically taking them outside whenever they need to relieve themselves. This sort of a routine is also a disciplined exercise that will help to reinforce in your puppy's mind, that you are the boss.

7. Rewarding Unwanted Behavior

Often humans make the mistake of accidentally rewarding unwanted behaviors, therefore, it is very important to recognize that any attention paid to an out of control, adolescent puppy, even negative attention, is likely going to be exciting and rewarding for your puppy.

Therefore, when you engage with an out of control Morkie puppy you end up actually rewarding them, which will encourage them to continue more of this unwanted behavior.

Be aware that chasing after a puppy when they have taken something they are not supposed to have, picking them up when they are barking or showing aggression, pushing them off when they jump on you or other people, or yelling when they refuse to come when called, are all forms of attention that can actually be rewarding for most puppies.

As your Morkie's guardian, it will be your responsibility to provide structure for your puppy, which will include finding acceptable and safe ways to allow your puppy to vent their energy without being destructive or harmful to others.

Activities that create or encourage an overly excited Morkie puppy, such as rough games of tug-o-war, or wild games of chase should be immediately curtailed, so that your puppy learns how to control their energy and play quietly and appropriately without jumping on everyone or engaging in barking or mouthy behavior.

Further, if your adolescent Morkie puppy displays excited energy simply from being petted by yourself, your family members or any visitors, you will need to teach yourself, your family and your friends to ignore your puppy until they calm down. Otherwise, you will be teaching your Morkie puppy that humans mean excitement.

For instance, when you continue to engage with an overly excited puppy, you are rewarding them for out of control behavior and literally teaching them that when they see humans, you want them to display excited energy.

Worse, once your puppy has learned that humans are a source of excitement, you will then have to work very long and hard to reverse this behavior.

Children are often a source of excitement that can cause an adolescent puppy to be extremely wound up. Do not allow your children to engage with an adolescent Morkie puppy unless you are there to supervise and teach the children appropriate and calm ways to interact with the puppy.

In order to keep everyone safe, it is very important that your Morkie puppy learn at an early age that neither children nor adults are sources of excitement.

You can help develop the minds of an adolescent Morkie and the minds of growing children at the same time by teaching children that your puppy needs structured walks and by showing them how to play fetch, search, hide and seek, or how to teach the Morkie puppy simple tricks and obedience skills that will be fun and positive interaction for everyone.

8. Back to Basics

When your puppy is going through what could be a belligerent and trying adolescence, when it seems that they have forgotten everything they may have learned so far, this is an especially good time to revisit the simple "Sit" command.

Now, to help re-establish your leadership role, you will want to ask your Morkie puppy to sit at every opportunity.

The simple act of "sitting" will help to calm an excited mind and will get your puppy's focus back on you.

9. Sit and More Sit

Every time you take your Morkie out for a walk, get into the habit of asking them to sit while you put on their leash — then sit and calmly wait while you put on your shoes or jacket — after you approach the door, ask them to sit again while you open the door — after you are on the other side of the door — ask them to sit again while you lock the door. If there are stairs or landings involved, ask them to sit at the top and also again at the bottom.

Every time you arrive at street intersection or crosswalk, ask your Morkie puppy to sit again, and do this in reverse when coming back home.

Also, every time you stop during your walk to speak to a neighbor, greet a friend or admire the view, ask your puppy to sit.

Every time you ask your young dog to sit for you, they are learning that you are the boss and that they must respect you as their leader.

Also, a sitting puppy is much more calm than one standing at the alert, ready to bolt.

Once your puppy is reliably sitting for you at least 50% of the time with voice command, also include the hand signal for "Sit", so that they will hear the word and also see the signal.

While you can use any hand signal, the universal hand signal for "Sit" is:

☑ Right arm (palm open facing upward) parallel to the floor, and then raising your arm, while bent at the elbow toward your right shoulder.

Once your Morkie is sitting reliable for you, remove the verbal "Sit" and replace it with the hand signal.

It's important to begin teaching hand signals during the adolescent stage of your puppy's life, because this will also help them to communicate in a way that is more natural to them — by watching you and feeling your energy, rather than always having to hear you speak a command.

As well, because the action of sitting helps to calm the mind of an excited puppy (or dog), teaching your puppy the "Sit" command a very important part of their daily interactions with your family members as well as people you may meet when out on a walk.

When you ask your puppy to "Sit" before you interact in any way with them, before you go out or in every door, before you feed them, etc., you are helping to quiet their mind, while making it more difficult for them to jump, lunge or bolt out a door.

The adolescent stage in a young dog's life is the perfect time to begin teaching hand signals for all your common commands, because they must look at you to understand what is expected of them, and when they are looking at you, they are more focused and less likely to take matters into their own paws.

10) Giving Up is Not an Option

Too often we humans get frustrated and give up on our dogs when they change from being the cute, cuddly and mostly obedient little puppy they once were, and become all kinds of trouble you never bargained for, as they grow into their adolescent stage.

Often times, it will be during the confusing adolescent stage of a dogs life that they find themselves abandoned and behind bars as their humans who promised to love and protect them, leave their once loved fur friends at the local pound or SPCA.

First of all, not all dogs go through a crazy adolescent period, and secondly, even if they do, please read this section carefully humans, because you can live through puppy adolescence and come out the other side relatively unscathed and a much more knowledgeable and patient guardian.

Congratulations are in order because you've been successful with potty training your young Morkie puppy and with teaching them to sleep in their own kennel at night. You've lived through the teething troubles, the chewing and the hand nipping and you no longer have to get up at 3:00 a.m. to let your puppy out to relieve themselves.

As well, you've taught your Morkie puppy their first few basic commands, and socialized them with many other dogs, people and places, so you should feel proud of your accomplishments and the leaps and bounds you and your puppy have accomplished together over the last several months.

Even though your adolescent puppy may be starting to act like a Tasmanian devil, and you may be having second thoughts, now is not the time to give up on them and yourself just because it may seem like someone switched your dog when you weren't looking.

Now is the time to remain consistent and persistent, and to know that you will eventually be able to enjoy the happy rewards of all your puppy raising diligence.

Yes, it can be quite a shock when what used to be your well behaved little darling who never chewed anything they weren't supposed to suddenly take it into their head to rip the stuffing out of your $3,000 couch or chew through a seat belt in your vehicle during the short 15 minutes you were shopping.

Even more disconcerting might be when your previously obedient and loving Morkie puppy who always listened to your directions suddenly appears to have gone deaf and can't remember their name when you expect them to follow you inside the house, and instead they take off running after a cat three blocks away.

And then, what happened to that quiet little puppy who never appeared to have a mean bone in their body who now spends most of their time at the window barking and growling at everything and everyone passing by?

Welcome to the world of canine adolescence where it appears that your puppy has turned into some sort of monster and all your previous hard work was for naught.

Of course, this dramatic switch from being the world's best puppy into the monster you can no longer control is not true for all puppies, as every puppy is unique.

However, being prepared for the worst will help you ride any impending storm and get you both out the other side where you can enjoy an even closer relationship than you previously had.

The adolescent phase may be very subtle for your Morkie puppy or on the other hand, it may be so dramatic that you're starting to feel guilty every time you drive past the local SPCA or dog pound because thoughts of rehoming are running through your head.

If you are at the stage with your puppy that you are having great difficulties and wondering if you made the right decision to share your home with a dog, rest assured that puppy adolescence is a normal phase of their development, which can be managed, and which will definitely pass.

As well, if you are finding yourself totally overwhelmed, there are many professionals who can provide valuable assistance to help you through this stage of your Morkie puppy's development.

For most puppies, adolescence will begin between the ages of five and seven months and this is also the time that you need to be making an appointment at your veterinarian's office to have your puppy spayed or neutered.

Although neutering or spaying will not prevent adolescent behavior entirely, it can certainly reduce the intensity of it, as during this period there are hormonal changes occurring that will affect your puppy's behavior.

While it's usually hormones that are the major cause of behavioral changes in your adolescent puppy, there are also physical changes occurring at the same time that you may not be aware of.

For instance, your puppy will be going through physical growth spurts which might be causing them some pain, as well as changes related to growth in their brain while your puppy's cerebral cortex becomes more involved in thinking for itself.

Usually, during this time of brain growth, a puppy will be trying to make choices on their own, and may not yet be capable of making the right choices and this is why their behavior can appear to be quite erratic.

During the early adolescent period of brain development in your Morkie puppy, the signals sometimes get mixed up and rerouted, which can result in the perplexing responses you might notice, when for instance, you ask you puppy to sit and they stare dumbly at you, even though they learned this command months ago.

Don't worry because your previous training will return.

11) Basic First Commands

All that's necessary for effectively teaching your puppy their basic first commands is a calm, consistent approach, combined with endless patience.

Most puppies are ready to begin training at about 10 to 12 weeks of age, however, be careful not to overdo it when they are under six months of age as their attention span will be short.

Make your training sessions no more than 5 or 10 minutes, positive and pleasant with lots of praise and/or treats so that your puppy will be looking forward to their next session.

Also, introduce the hand signals that go along with the verbal commands so that once they learn both, you can remove the verbal commands and only use hand signals.

a) Come

While most puppies are capable of learning commands and tricks, the first and most important command you need to teach your puppy is the recall, or *"Come"* command.

The hand signal for "Come" is your arms spread wide open. This is a command they can see from a great distance.

Begin the "Come" command inside your home. Go into a larger room, such as your living room area. Place your puppy in front of you, attach their leash or a longer line to their collar, while you back away from them a few feet.

Say the command "Come" in an excited voice and hold your arms open wide. If they do not immediately come to you, gently give a tug on the leash so that they understand that they are supposed to move toward you. When they come to you praise them and give a treat they really enjoy.

Once your puppy can accomplish a "Come" command almost every time inside your home, you can then graduate them to a nearby park or quiet outside area where you will repeat the process.

You may want to purchase an extra long line (25 or 50 feet) so that you are always attached to your Morkie puppy and can encourage them in the right direction should they become distracted.

b) Sit

The "Sit" and "Stay" commands are both easy commands to teach that will help to keep your Morkie puppy safe and out of danger in most every circumstance. Find a quiet time to teach these commands when your puppy is not overly tired.

Ask your puppy to "Sit" and if they do not yet understand the command, show them what you mean by gently squeezing with your thumb and middle finger, the area across the back that joins with their back legs. Do not just push them down into a sit as this can cause damage to their back or joints. When they sit, give them a treat and praise them.

When you say the word "Sit", at the same time show them the hand signal for this command, which is bending your arm at the elbow and raising your right hand, palm open facing upward, toward your shoulder.

c) Stay

Once your Morkie puppy can reliably "Sit", say the word "Stay" and hold your outstretched arm, palm open toward their head and back away a few steps.

If they try to follow, calmly say "No" and put them back into "Sit". Give a treat and then say again, "Stay" with the hand signal and back away a few steps.

Once your puppy is sitting and staying, you can then ask them to "Come". Don't forget to use the open arms hand signal for "Come." Be a little excited with the "Come" command so that your puppy will always enjoy correctly responding and immediately returning to you.

Practice these three basic commands everywhere you go, and use the "Sit" command every time you go for a walk, before you open the door, after you are on the other side of the door, before you go down the stairs, once you are at the bottom of the stairs, and every time you stop when you are on your walk, and pretty soon you will have a puppy who automatically sits whenever you stop moving.

As your puppy gets older, and their attention span increases, you will be able to train for longer periods of time.

12. Hand Signals

Hand signal training is by far the most useful and efficient training method for every dog, including the Morkie.

This is because all too often we inundate our canine companions with a great deal of chatter and noise that they really do not understand because English is not their first language.

Contrary to what some humans might think, the first language of a Morkie, or any dog, is a combination of sensing energy and watching body language, which requires no spoken word or sound.

Therefore, when we humans take the time to teach our dog hand signals for all their basic commands, we are communicating with them at a level they instinctively understand, plus we are helping them to become great followers, as they must watch us to understand what is required of them.

a) Come

When first teaching hand signals to your Morkie, always show the hand signal for the command at the same time you say the word. If they are totally ignoring the command, it will be time to incorporate a lunge line, which is a very long leash to help you teach the "Come" command.

> ☑ **Come:** you can kneel down for this command or stay standing. Open your arms wide like you are hugging a very large tree. This hand signal can be seen from a long distance.

Simply attach a 20 foot line to their collar and let them sniff about in a large yard or at your neighborhood park.

At your leisure, firmly ask them to "Come" and show the hand signal. If they do not immediately come to you, give a firm tug with the lunge line, so that they understand what you are asking of them.

If they still do not "Come" toward you, simply reel them in until they are in front of you. Then let them wander about again, until you are ready to ask them to "Come".

Repeat this process until your Morkie responds correctly at least 80% of the time. You can also reinforce the command by giving a treat when they come back to you when asked. Always ask them to "Sit" when they return to you.

b) Sit

✅ **Sit**: right arm (palm open facing upward) parallel to the floor, and then raise your arm, while bent at the elbow toward your shoulder.

Sit is a very simple, yet extremely valuable command for all puppies and dogs.

If your dog is not sitting on command, try holding a treat above and slightly behind their head, so that when they look up for it they may automatically sit to see it.

Slowly remove the treats as reward and replace the treat with a "life reward", such as a chest rub or a thumbs up signal and your smile.

If your Morkie is not particularly treat motivated, lift up and slightly back on the leash when asking them to sit (stand in front of them), and if they still are having difficulties, reach down with your free hand, place it across your dog's back at the place where the back legs join the hip and gently squeeze.

Do NOT simply push down on your dog's back to force their hind legs to collapse under them as this pressure could harm their spine or leg joints.

c) Stay

> ☑ **Stay**: right armed fully extended toward your dog's head, palm open, hand bent up at the wrist.

Once your Morkie is in the "Sit" position, ask them to "Stay" with both the verbal cue and the hand signal.

TIP: if you are right-handed, use your right arm and hand for the signal, and if you are left-handed, use your left arm and hand for the signal. Using your dominant hand will be much more effective because your strongest energy emanates from the palm of your dominant hand.

While your dog is sitting and staying, slowly back away from them. If they move from their position, calmly put them back into sit and ask them to "Stay" again, using both the verbal cue and the hand signal.

Continue to practice this until your dog understands that you want them to stay sitting and not move toward you.

With all commands, when your Morkie is just learning, be patient and always reward them with a treat and your happy praise for a job well done.

13. Simple Tricks

When teaching your Morkie tricks, in order to give them extra incentive, find a treat that they really like, and give the treat as rewards and to help solidify a good performance. Most dogs will be extra attentive during training sessions when they know that they will be rewarded with their favorite treats.

If your Morkie is less than six months old when you begin teaching them tricks, keep your training sessions short (no more than 5 or 10 minutes) and fun, and as they become adults, you can extend your sessions as they will be able to maintain their focus for longer periods of time.

a) Shake a Paw

Who doesn't love a dog that knows how to shake a paw? This is one of the easiest tricks to teach your Morkie.

TIP: most dogs are naturally either right or left pawed. If you know which paw your dog favors, ask them to shake this paw.

Find a quiet place to practice, without noisy distractions or other pets, and stand or sit in front of your dog. Place them in the sitting position and have a treat in your left hand.

Say the command *"Shake"* while putting your right hand behind their left or right paw and pulling the paw gently toward yourself until you are holding their paw in your hand. Immediately praise them and give them the treat.

Most dogs will learn the "Shake" trick very quickly, and very soon, once you put out your hand, your Morkie will immediately lift their paw and put it into your hand, without your assistance or any verbal cue.

Practice every day until they are 100% reliable with this trick, and then it will be time to add another trick to their repertoire.

b) Roll Over

You will find that just like your Morkie is naturally either right or left pawed, that they will also naturally want to roll either to the right or the left side. Take advantage of this by asking your dog to roll to the side they naturally prefer.

Sit with your dog on the floor and put them in a lie down position. Hold a treat in your hand and place it close to their nose without allowing them to grab it, and while they are in the lying position, move the treat to the right or left side of their head so that they have to roll over to get to it.

You will very quickly see which side they want to naturally roll to, and once you see this, move the treat to this side. Once they roll over to this side, immediately give them the treat and praise them.

You can say the verbal cue *"Over"* while you demonstrate the hand signal motion (moving your right hand in a circular motion) or moving the treat from one side of their head to the other with a half circle motion.

Once your Morkie can roll over every time you ask, it will be time to teach them another trick.

c) Sit Pretty

While this trick is a little more complicated, and most dogs pick up on it very quickly, remember that every dog is different so always exercise patience.

Find a quiet space with few distractions and sit or stand in front of your dog and ask them to "Sit".

Have a treat nearby (on a countertop or table) and when they sit, use both of your hands to lift up their front paws into the sitting pretty position, while saying the command *"Sit Pretty"*. Help them balance in this position while you praise them and give them the treat.

Once your Morkie can do the balancing part of the trick quite easily without your help, sit or stand in front of your dog while asking them to *"Sit Pretty"* and hold the treat above their head, at the level their nose would be when they sit pretty.

If they attempt to stand on their back legs to get the treat, you may be holding the treat too high, which will encourage them to stand on their back legs to reach it. Go back to the first step and put them back into the *"Sit"* position and again lift their paws while their backside remains on the floor.

The hand signal for *"Sit Pretty"* is a straight arm held over your dog's head with a closed fist.

Make this a fun and entertaining time for your Morkie and practice a few times every day until they can *"Sit Pretty"* on hand signal command every time you ask.

A young Morkie puppy should be able to easily learn these basic tricks before they are six months old and when you are patient and make your training sessions short and fun for your dog, they will be eager to learn more.

14. Adult Training

When your Morkie is a full grown adult (approximately two years of age), now is the time that you can begin more complicated or advanced training sessions. They will enjoy it and when you have the desire and patience, there is no end to the tricks you can teach a willing Morkie.

For instance, you may wish to teach your adult Morkie more advanced tricks, such as how to dance, or the opposite paw shake or side roll over, which are more difficult than you might expect.

If you and your Morkie are really enjoying learning new tricks together, you might want to advance to teaching them the *"commando crawl"*, how to *"speak"* or to *"jump through the human hoop"*. All of these tricks are fun to teach and will exercise both your Morkie's body and mind.

As well, the more control you have over your Morkie, the easier it will be to teach them a fun sport, such as Agility.

The only restriction to how far you can go with training your adult Morkie will be your imagination and their personal ability or desire to perform.

Chapter 15: Poisonous Foods & Plants

1. Poisonous Foods

While some dogs are smart enough not to want to eat foods that can harm or kill them, other canine companions will eat absolutely anything they can get their teeth on.

As conscientious guardians for our fur friends, it will always be our responsibility to make certain that when we share our homes with a dog, we never leave foods that could be toxic or lethal to them easily within their reach.

While there are many foods that can be toxic to a Morkie, the following alphabetical list contains some of the more common foods that can seriously harm or even kill our dogs including:

Bread Dough: if your dog eats bread dough, their body heat will cause the dough to rise inside the stomach. As the dough expands during the rising process, alcohol is produced.

Dogs who have eaten bread dough may experience stomach bloating, abdominal pain, vomiting, disorientation and depression. Because bread dough can rise to many times its size, eating only a small amount will cause a problem for any dog.

Broccoli: the toxic ingredient in broccoli is isothiocynate. While it may cause stomach upset, it probably won't be very harmful unless the amount eaten is more than 10% of the dog's total daily diet.

Chocolate: contains theobromine, a chemical that is toxic to dogs in large enough quantities. Chocolate also contains caffeine, which is found in coffee, tea, and certain soft drinks. Different types of chocolate contain different amounts of theobromine and caffeine.

For example, dark chocolate and baking chocolate or cocoa powder contain more of these compounds than milk chocolate does, therefore, a dog would need to eat more milk chocolate in order to become ill.

However, even a few ounces of chocolate can be enough to cause illness or death in a small dog like the Morkie, therefore, no amount or type of chocolate should be considered safe for a dog to eat.

Chocolate toxicity can cause vomiting, diarrhea, rapid or irregular heart rate, restlessness, muscle tremors, and seizures. Death can occur within 24 hours of eating.

During many holidays such as Christmas, New Year's, Valentine's, Easter and Halloween, chocolate is often more easily accessible to curious dogs, especially from children who are not so careful with where they keep their Halloween stash and who are an easy mark for a hungry dog.

In some cases, people unwittingly poison their dogs by offering them chocolate as a treat or leaving a luscious chocolate frosted cake easily within licking distance when nobody is looking.

Caffeine: beverages containing caffeine (like soda, tea, coffee, chocolate) act as a stimulant and can accelerate your dog's heartbeat to a dangerous level. Dogs eating caffeine have been known to have seizures, some of which are fatal.

Cooked Bones: can be extremely hazardous for a dog because the bones become brittle when cooked which causes them to splinter when the dog chews on them.

The splinters have sharp edges that have been known to become stuck in the teeth, and cause choking when caught in the throat or cause a rupture or puncture of the stomach lining or intestinal tract.

Especially dangerous are cooked turkey and chicken legs, ham, pork chop and veal bones. Symptoms of choking include:

- Pale or blue gums
- Gasping open-mouthed breathing
- Pawing at the face
- Slow, shallow breathing
- Unconscious, with dilated pupils

Grapes and Raisins: can cause acute (sudden) kidney failure in dogs. While it is unknown what the toxic agent is in this fruit, clinical signs can occur within 24 hours of eating and include vomiting, diarrhea, and lethargy (tiredness).

Other signs of illness caused from eating grapes or raisins relate to the eventual shutdown of kidney functioning.

Garlic and Onions: contain chemicals that damage red blood cells by rupturing them so that they lose their ability to carry oxygen effectively, which leaves the dog short of oxygen, causing what is called *"hemolytic anemia"*.

Poisoning can occur with a single ingestion of large quantities of garlic or onions or with repeated meals containing small amounts.

Cooking does not reduce the potential toxicity of onions and garlic.

NOTE: fresh, cooked, and/or powdered garlic or onions are commonly found in baby food, which is sometimes given to dogs when they are sick, therefore, be certain to carefully read food labels before feeding to your Morkie.

Macadamia Nuts: are commonly found in candies and chocolates. Although the mechanism of macadamia nut toxicity is not well understood, the clinical signs in dogs having eaten these nuts include depression, weakness, vomiting, tremors, joint pain, and pale gums.

Signs can occur within 12 hours after eating. In some cases, symptoms can resolve themselves without treatment within 24 to 48 hours, however, keeping a close eye on your Morkie will be strongly recommended.

Mushrooms: mushroom poisoning can be fatal if certain species of mushrooms are eaten.

The most commonly reported severely toxic species of mushroom in the US is Amanita phalloides (Death Cap mushroom), which is also quite a common species found in most parts of Britain. Other Amanita species are also toxic.

This deadly mushroom is often found growing in grassy or wooded area near various deciduous and coniferous trees, which means that if you're out walking with your Morkie in the woods, they could easily find these mushrooms.

Eating them can cause severe liver disease and neurological disorders. If you suspect your dog has eaten these mushrooms, immediately take them to your veterinarian, as the recommended treatment is to induce vomiting and to give activated charcoal. Further treatment for liver disease may also be necessary.

Pits and Seeds: many seeds and pits found in a variety of fruits, including apples, apricots, cherries, pears and plums, contain cyanogenic glycosides that can cause cyanide poisoning in your Morkie.

The symptoms of cyanide poisoning usually occur within 15-20 minutes to a few hours after eating and symptoms can include initial excitement, followed by rapid respiration rate, salivation, voiding of urine and feces, vomiting, muscle spasm, staggering, and coma before death.

Dogs suffering from cyanide poisoning that live more than 2 hours after onset of symptoms will usually recover.

Raw Salmon or Trout: Salmon Poisoning Disease (SPD), can be a problem for anyone who feeds their dog a raw meat diet that includes raw salmon or trout. The cause is infection by a rickettsial organism called Neorickettsia helminthoeca.

Nanophyteus salmincola are found to infect some species of freshwater snails. The infected snail is eaten by the fish as part of the food chain. The dog is exposed only when it eats an infected fish.

A sudden onset of symptoms occur 5-7 days after eating the infected fish. In the acute stages, gastrointestinal symptoms are quite similar to canine parvovirus.

SPD has a mortality rate of up to 90%, can be diagnosed with a fecal sample and is treatable if caught in time.

Prevention is simple, cook all fish before feeding it to your Morkie and immediately see your veterinarian if you suspect that your dog has eaten raw salmon or trout.

Tobacco: all forms of tobacco, including patches, nicotine gum and chewing tobacco can be fatal to dogs if eaten.

Signs of poisoning can appear within an hour and include hyperactivity, salivation, panting, vomiting and diarrhea. Advanced signs include muscle weakness, twitching, collapse, coma, increased heart rate and eventually cardiac arrest.

Never leave tobacco products within reach of your Morkie, and if you suspect your dog has eaten any of these, seek immediate veterinary help.

Tomatoes: contain atropine, which can cause dilated pupils, tremors and irregular heartbeat. The highest concentration of atropine is found in the leaves and stems of tomato plants, next is the unripe (green) tomatoes, followed by the ripe tomato.

Xylitol: is an artificial sweetener found in products such as gum, candy, mints, toothpaste, and mouthwash that is recognized by the National Animal Poison Control Center to be a risk to dogs.

Xylitol is harmful to dogs because it causes a sudden release of insulin in the body that leads to hypoglycemia (low blood sugar). Xylitol can also cause liver damage in dogs.

Within 30 minutes after eating a product containing xylitol, the dog may vomit, be lethargic (tired), and/or be uncoordinated. However, some signs of toxicity can also be delayed for hours or even for a few days. Xylitol toxicity in dogs can be fatal if left untreated.

Please be aware that the above list is just some of the more common foods that can be toxic or fatal to our fur friends and that there are other foods we should never be feeding our dogs.

If you have one of those dogs who will happily eat anything that looks or smells even slightly like food, be certain to keep these foods far away from your beloved Morkie and you'll help them to live a long and healthy life.

2. Poisonous Household Plants

Many common house plants are actually poisonous to our canine companions, and although many dogs simply will ignore house plants, some will attempt to eat anything, especially puppies who want to taste everything in their new world.

More than 700 plant species contain toxins that may harm or be fatal to puppies or dogs depending on the size of the puppy or dog and how much they may eat. It will be especially important to be aware of the more common household plants when you are sharing your home with a new puppy. Following is a short list of the more common household plants, what they look like, the different names they are known by, and what symptoms would be apparent if your puppy or dog decides to eat them.

Aloe Plant: (medicine plant or Barbados aloe), is a very common succulent that is toxic to dogs. The toxic agent in this plant is Aloin. The bitter yellow substance is found in most aloe species and may cause vomiting and/or reddish urine.

Asparagus Fern: (emerald feather, emerald fern, sprengeri fern, plumosa fern, lace fern). The toxic agent in this plant is sapogenin — a steroid found in a variety of plants. Berries of this plant cause vomiting, diarrhea and/or abdominal pain or (skin inflammation) from repeated exposure.

Corn Plant: (cornstalk plant, dracaena, dragon tree, ribbon plant) is toxic to dogs. Saponin is the offensive chemical compound found in this plant. If the plant is eaten, vomiting (with or without blood), loss of appetite, depression and/or increased salivation can occur.

Cyclamen: (Sowbread) is a pretty, flowering plant that, if eaten, can cause increased salivation, vomiting and diarrhea. If a dog eats a large amount of the plant's tubers, which are usually found below the soil at the root — heart rhythm abnormalities, seizures and even death can occur.

Dieffenbachia: (dumb cane, tropic snow, exotica) contains a chemical that is a poisonous deterrent to animals. If the plant is eaten, oral irritation can occur, especially on the tongue and lips. This irritation can lead to increased salivation, difficulty swallowing and vomiting.

Elephant Ear: (caladium, taro, pai, ape, cape, via, via sori, malanga) contains a chemical similar to that found in dieffenbachia, therefore, an dog's toxic reaction to elephant ear is similar: oral irritation, increased salivation, difficulty swallowing and vomiting.

Heartleaf Philodendron: (horsehead philodendron, cordatum, fiddle leaf, panda plant, split-leaf philodendron, fruit salad plant, red emerald, red princess, saddle leaf), is a common, easy-to-grow houseplant that contains a chemical irritating to the mouth, tongue and lips of dogs. An affected dog may also experience increased salivation, vomiting and difficulty swallowing.

JadePlant: (baby jade, dwarf rubber plant, jade tree, Chinese rubber plant, Japanese rubber plant, friendship tree). While the toxic property in this plant is unknown, eating it can cause depression, loss of coordination and, although more rare, slow heart rate.

Lilies: some plants of the lily family are toxic to dogs. The peace lily (also known as Mauna Loa) is toxic to dogs. Eating the peace lily or calla lily can cause irritation of the tongue and lips, increased salivation, difficulty swallowing and vomiting.

Satin Pothos: (silk pothos), if eaten by a dog, the plant may cause irritation to the mouth, lips and tongue, while the dog may also experience increased salivation, vomiting and/or difficulty swallowing.

The plants noted above are only a few of the more common household plants, and every conscientious Morkie guardian will want to educate themselves before bringing plants into the home that could be toxic to their canine companions.

3. Poison Proof Your Home

You can learn about many potentially toxic and poisonous sources both inside and outside your home by visiting the ASPCA Animal Poison Control Center website.

Always keep your veterinarian's emergency number in a place where you can quickly access it, as well as the Emergency Poison Control telephone number, in case you suspect that your dog may have been poisoned.

Knowing what to do if you suspect your dog may have been poisoned and being able to quickly contact the right people could save your Morkie's life.

If you keep toxic cleaning substances (including fertilizers and vehicle products) in your home or garage, always keep them behind closed doors. As well, keep any medications where your Morkie can never get to them, and seriously consider eliminating the use of any and all toxic products, for the health of both yourself and your best friend.

4. Garden Plants

Please note that there are also many outdoor plants that can be toxic or poisonous to your Morkie, therefore, always check what plants are growing in your garden and if any may be harmful, remove them or make certain that your Morkie puppy or adult dog cannot eat them.

Cornell University, Department of Animal Science lists many different categories of poisonous plants affecting dogs , including house plants, flower garden plants, vegetable garden plants, plants found in swamps or moist areas, plants found in fields, trees and shrubs, plants found in wooded areas, and ornamental plants.

5. Grass

Also, be aware that many puppies and adult dogs will eat grass, just because. Perhaps they are bored, or need a little fiber in their diet. Remember that canines are natural scavengers always on the look out for something they can eat, and so long as the grass is healthy and has not been sprayed with toxic chemicals, this should not be a concern.

6. Animal Poison Control Centre

The ASPCA Animal Poison Control Center is staffed 24 hours a day, 365 days a year and is a valuable resource for learning about what plants are toxic and possibly poisonous to your dog.

Poison Emergency USA

Call: 1 (888) 426-4435

When calling the Poison Emergency number, a $65. US (£39.42) consultation fee may be applied to your credit card.

Poison Emergency UK

- Call Pet Poison Helpline 800-213-6680 (payable service)

- Call RSPCA 0300 1234 999

www.aspca.org = ASPCA Poison Control. Animal Poison Control.

Chapter 16: Caring for Aging Dogs

1. What to Be Aware Of

As a result of advances in veterinarian care, improvements in diet and nutrition and general knowledge concerning proper care of our canine companions, our dogs are able to enjoy longer, healthier lives, and as such, when caring for them we need to be aware of behavioral and physical changes that will affect our dogs as they approach old age.

A Morkie will be entering their senior years at around age 8 to 10 years of age.

a) Physiological Changes

As our beloved canine companions become senior dogs, they will be suffering from very similar, physical aging problems that affect us humans, such as pain, stiffness and arthritis, diminished or complete loss of hearing and sight and inability to control their bowels and bladder. Any of these problems will reduce a dog's willingness to want to exercise.

b) Behavioral Changes

Further, a senior Morkie may experience behavioral changes resulting from loss of hearing and sight, such as disorientation, fear or startle reactions and overall grumpiness from any number of physical problems that could be causing them pain whenever they move.

Just as research and science has improved our human quality of life in our senior years, the same is becoming true for our canine counterparts who are able to benefit from dietary supplements and pharmaceutical products to help them be as comfortable as possible in their advancing years.

Of course there will be some inconveniences associated with keeping a dog with advancing years around the home, however, your Morkie deserves no less than to spend their final days in your loving care after they have unconditionally given you their entire lives.

c) Geriatric Dogs

Being aware of the changes that are likely occurring in a senior dog will help you to better care for them during their geriatric years.

For instance, most dogs will experience hearing loss and visual impairment, and depending upon which goes first (hearing or sight). If a dog's hearing is compromised, then using more hand signals will be helpful.

Deaf dogs will still be able to hear louder noises and feel vibrations, therefore hand clapping, using a loud clicker or stomping your foot on the floor may be a way to get their attention.

If a senior dog loses their eyesight, most dogs will still be able to easily navigate their familiar surroundings, and you will only need to be extra watchful on their behalf when taking them to unfamiliar territory. If they still have their hearing, you will be able to assist your dog with verbal cues and commands.

Dogs that have lost both their hearing and their sight will need to be close to you so that they can relax and not feel nervous, and so that you can communicate by touching parts of their body.

Generally speaking, even when a dog becomes blind and/or deaf, their powerful sense of smell is still functioning, which means that they will be able to tell where you are and navigate their environment by using their nose.

d) More Bathroom Breaks

Bathroom breaks may need to become more frequent in older dogs who may lose their ability to hold it for longer periods of time, so be prepared to be more watchful and to offer them opportunities to go outside more frequently during the day.

You may also want to place a pee pad near the door, in case they just can't hold it long enough, or if you have not already taught them to bathroom on an indoor potty patch, or pee pad, now may be the time for this alternative bathroom arrangement.

A dog who has been house trained for years will feel the shame and upset of not being able to hold it long enough to get to their regular bathroom location, so be kind and do whatever you need to do to help them not to have to feel bad about failing bowel or bladder control.

Our beloved canine companions may also begin to show signs of cognitive decline and changes in the way their brain functions, similar to what happens to humans suffering from Alzheimer's, where they start to wander about aimlessly, sometimes during the middle of the night. Make sure that if this is happening with your Morkie at nighttime, that they cannot accidentally harm themselves.

Being aware that an aging Morkie will be experiencing many symptoms that are similar to an aging human, will help you to understand how best to keep them safe and as comfortable as possible during this golden age in their lives.

2. How to Make Them Comfortable

a) Regular Checkups

During this time in your Morkie's life, when their immune systems become weakened and they may be experiencing pain, you will want to get into the habit of taking your senior Morkie for regular veterinarian checkups. Take them for a veterinarian checkup every six months so that early detection of any problems can quickly be attended to and solutions for helping to keep your aging Morkie comfortable can be provided.

b) No Rough Play

An older Morkie will not have the same energy or willingness to play that they did when they were younger, therefore, do not allow younger children to rough house with an older dog. Explain to them that the dog is getting older and that as a result they must learn to be gentle and to leave the dog alone when it may want to rest or sleep.

c) Mild Exercise

Dogs still love going for walks, even when they are getting older and slowing down. Although an older Morkie will generally have less energy, they still need to exercise and keep moving, and taking them out regularly for shorter walks will keep them healthier and happier long into old age.

d) Best Quality Food

Everyone has heard the saying, *"you are what you eat"* and for a senior dog, what they eat is even more important as their digestive system may no longer be functioning at peak performance. Therefore, feeding a high quality, protein-based food will be important for their continued health.

As well, if your older Morkie is overweight, you will want to help them shed excess pounds so that they will not be placing undue stress on their joints or heart, and the best way to do this is by feeding smaller quantities of a higher quality food.

e) Clean and Parasite Free

The last thing an aging Morkie should have to deal with is the misery of itching and scratching, so make sure that you continue to give them regular baths with the appropriate shampoos and conditioners to keep their coat and skin comfortable and free from parasites.

f) Plenty of Water

Proper hydration is essential for helping to keep an older Morkie comfortable. Water is life giving for every creature, so make certain that your aging dog has easy access to plenty of clean, fresh water which will help to improve their energy and digestion and also prevent dehydration which can add to joint stiffness.

g) Keeping Warm

Just as older humans feel the cold more, so do older dogs. Keeping your senior Morkie warm will help to alleviate some of the pain of their joint stiffness or arthritis. Make sure their bed or kennel is not kept in a drafty location and perhaps consider a heated bed for them.

Be aware that your aging Morkie will be more sensitive to extremes in temperature, and it will be up to you to make sure that they are comfortable at all times, which means not too hot and not too cold.

h) Indoor Clothing

We humans tend to wear warmer clothing as we get older, simply because we have more difficulty maintaining a comfortable body temperature and the same will be true of our senior Morkie companions.

Therefore, while you most likely already have a selection of outdoor clothing appropriate to the climate in which you live, you may not have considered keeping your Morkie warm while inside the home. Now would be the time to consider doggy t-shirts or sweater clothing options to help keep your aging companion comfortably warm both inside and out.

i) Steps or Stairs

If your Morkie is allowed to sleep on the human couch or chair, but they are having difficulties getting up there as their joints are becoming stiff and painful, consider buying them a set of foam stairs so that they do not have to make the jump to their favorite sleeping place.

j) Comfortable Bed

While most dogs seem to be happy with sleeping on the floor, providing them with a padded, soft bed will greatly help to relieve sore spots and joint pain in older dogs.

If there is a draft in the home, generally it will be at floor level, therefore, a bed that is raised up off of the floor will be warmer for your senior Morkie who will be much more comfortable sleeping in a cozy dog bed.

k) More Love and Attention

Last, but not least, make sure that you give your senior Morkie lots of love and attention and never leave them alone for long periods of time.

When they are not feeling their best, they will want to be with you all that much more because you are their guardian whom they trust and love beyond life itself.

3. What is Euthanasia?

Every veterinarian will have received special training to help provide all incurably ill, injured or aged pets who have come to the end of their natural lives with a humane and gentle death, through a process called *"euthanasia"*.

When the time comes, euthanasia, or putting a dog *"to sleep"*, will usually be a two-step process.

First, the veterinarian will inject the dog with a sedative to make them sleepy, calm and comfortable.

Second, the veterinarian will inject a special drug that will peacefully stop their heart. These drugs work in such a way that the dog will not experience any awareness whatsoever that their life is ending. What they will experience is very much like what we humans experience when going under anesthesia during a surgical procedure.

Once the second stage drug has been injected, the entire process takes about 10 to 20 seconds, at which time the veterinarian will then check to make certain that the dog's heart has stopped.

There is no suffering with this process, which is a very gentle and humane way to end a dog's suffering and allow them to peacefully pass on.

4. When to Help a Dog Transition

The impending loss of a beloved dog is one of the most painfully difficult and emotionally devastating coping experiences a canine guardian will ever have to face.

For the sake of our faithful companions, because we do not want to prolong their suffering, we humans will have to do our best to look at our dog's situation practically, rather than emotionally, so that we can make the best decision for them.

They may be suffering from extreme old age and the inability to even walk outside to relieve themselves, and thus suffering the indignity of regularly soiling their sleeping area, or they may have been diagnosed with an incurable illness that is causing them much pain, or they may have been seriously injured.

Whatever the reason for a canine companion's suffering, it will be up to their human guardian to calmly guide the end-of-life experience so that any further discomfort and distress can be minimized.

a) When There is Uncertainty

In circumstances where it is not entirely clear how much a dog is suffering, it will be helpful to pay close attention to your Morkie's behavior and keep a daily log or record so that you can know for certain how much of their day is difficult and painful for them, and how much is not.

When you keep a daily log, it will be easier to decide if the dog's quality of life has become so poor that it makes better sense to offer them the gift of peacefully going to sleep. During this time of uncertainty, it will also be very important to discuss with a veterinarian what signs of suffering may be associated with the dog's particular disease or condition, so that you know what to look for.

Often a dog may still continue to eat or drink despite being distraught, having difficulty breathing, excessively panting, being disoriented or in much pain, and as their caring guardians, we will have to weigh their love of eating against how much they are really suffering in all other aspects of their life.

Obviously, if a canine guardian can clearly see that their beloved companion is suffering throughout their days and nights, it will make sense to help humanely end their suffering by planning a euthanasia procedure.

We humans are often tempted to delay the inevitable moment of euthanasia, because we love our dogs so much and cannot bear the anticipation of the intense grief we know will overwhelm us when we must say our final goodbyes to our beloved fur friend.

Unfortunately, we may regret that we allowed our dog to suffer too long, and find ourselves wishing that if only we humans had the same option, to peacefully let go, when we reach such a stage in our own lives.

5. Grieving a Lost Pet

Often we humans do not fully recognize the terrible grief involved in losing a beloved canine friend. There will be many who do not understand the close bond we humans can have with our dogs, which is often unlike any we have with our human counterparts.

Your friends may give you pitying looks and try to cheer you up, but if they have never experienced such a loss themselves, they may also secretly think you are making too much fuss over "just a dog".

For some of us humans, the loss of a beloved dog is so painful that they decide never to share their lives with another, because they cannot bear the thought of going through the pain of loss again.

Expect to feel terribly sad, tearful and yes, depressed because those who are close to their canine companions will feel their loss no less acutely than the loss of a human friend or life partner. The grieving process can take some time to recover from, and some of us never totally recover.

After the loss of a family dog, first you need to take care of yourself by making certain that you keep eating and getting regular sleep, even though you will feel an almost eerie sense of loneliness.

Losing a beloved dog is a shock to the system, which can also affect your concentration and your ability to find joy or want to participate in other activities that may be part of the rest of your life.

During this early grieving time you will need to take extra care while driving or performing tasks that require your concentration as you may find yourself distracted.

If there are other dogs or pets in the home, they will also be grieving the loss of a companion, and may display this by acting depressed, being off their food or showing little interest in play or games. Therefore, you need to help guide your other pets through this grieving process by keeping them busy and interested, taking them for extra walks and spending more time with them.

Many people do not wait long enough before attempting to replace a lost pet and will immediately go to the local shelter and rescue a deserving dog. While this may help to distract you from your grieving process, this is not really fair to the new fur member of your family.

Bringing a new pet into a home that is depressed and grieving the loss of a long time canine member may create behavioral problems for the new dog who will be faced with learning all about their new home while also dealing with the unstable energy of the grieving family.

A better scenario would be to allow yourself the time to properly grieve by waiting a minimum of one month to allow yourself and your family to feel happier and more stable before deciding upon sharing your home with another dog.

The grieving process will be different for everyone and you will know when the time is right to consider sharing your home with another canine companion.

6. The Rainbow Bridge Poem

"Just this side of heaven
is a place called Rainbow Bridge.

When an animal dies that has been
especially close to someone here,
that pet goes to Rainbow Bridge.
There are meadows and hills for all of our special friends
so they can run and play together.
There is plenty of food, water and sunshine,
and our friends are warm and comfortable.

All the animals who had been ill and old
are restored to health and vigor;

those who were hurt or maimed
are made whole and strong again,
just as we remember them in our dreams
of days and times gone by.
The animals are happy and content,
except for one small thing;
they each miss someone very special to them,
who had to be left behind.

They all run and play together,
but the day comes when one suddenly stops
and looks into the distance.
His bright eyes are intent; His eager body quivers. Suddenly he
begins to run from the group,
flying over the green grass,
his legs carrying him faster and faster.

You have been spotted,
and when you and your special friend finally meet,
you cling together in joyous reunion,
never to be parted again.
The happy kisses rain upon your face;
your hands again caress the beloved head,
and you look once more into the trusting eyes
of your pet, so long gone from your life
but never absent from your heart.

Then you cross Rainbow Bridge together...."

- Author unknown

7. Memorials

There are as many unique ways to honor the passing of a beloved pet as each of our fur friends is unique and special to us.

For instance, you may wish to have your fur friend cremated and preserve their ashes in a special urn or sprinkle their ashes along their favorite walk.

Perhaps you will want to have a special marker, photo bereavement, photo engraved Rainbow Bridge Poem, or wooden plaque created in honor of your lost friend.

You may wish to keep their memory close to you at all times by having a DNA remembrance pendant or bracelet designed.

As well, there are support groups, such as Rainbow Bridge, which is a grief support community, to help you and your family through this painful period of loss and grief.

Chapter 17: Rescue Organizations

When you are considering rescuing a specific breed or cross breed of dog or puppy, the first place to start your search will be with your local shelter and rescue groups.

1. Shelters

Here you can expect to pay an adoption fee to cover the cost of spaying or neutering, but this will be only a small percentage of what you would pay a breeder, and you will be saving a life at the same time, without supporting puppy mills.

2. Online Resources

Sites such as Petango, Adopt A Pet and Pet Finder can be good places to begin your search.

Each of these online resources are a central gathering site for hundreds and hundreds of local shelters, humane societies and rescue groups.

3. Canine Clubs

Another place to search will be Yorkshire Terrier and Maltese Clubs in your local area. These groups may often have rescue dogs available, including a Morkie crossbreed.

Chapter 18: Resources & References

The following resources and references are listed alphabetically within their specific category.

1. Poison Control

ASPCA Poison Control
www.aspca.org

2. Breeders, Registries & Rescues

Adopt A Pet
www.adoptapet.com

American Canine Hybrid Club
www.achclub.com

American Maltese Association
www.americanmaltese.org

Canine Registry
www.designercanineregistry.com

Designer Dogs - The Kennel Club
www.thekennelclub.org.uk

International Designer Canine Registry®
www.designercanineregistry.com

Little Rascals
www.littlerascaluk.com

Mini Pups Breeder
www.minipups.ca

Morkie Puppies
www.morkiepuppies.net

Morkies and Morkie Poo Pups
www.morkiesandmorkiespoos.com

National Hybrid Registry
www.nationalhybridregistry.com]

Petango
www.petango.com

Pet Finder
www.petfinder.com [

Poisonous Plants Affecting Dogs - Cornell University,
Department of Animal Science
www.ansci.cornell.edu/plants/dogs

Yorkshire Terrier and Toy Breed Rescue
www.yorkieandtoybreedrescue.co.uk

Yorkie Haven Rescue
www.yorkiehavenrescue.com

3. Equipment and Supplies

Andis Dog Clippers [andis.com]
www.andis.com

Dog Bowl for Your Dog
www.dogbowlforyourdog.com

Dremel™ Nail Grinder for Dogs
Modern Puppies
www.modernpuppies.com

Oster Dog Clippers
www.osterpro.com

Remove Urine Odors
www.removeurineodors.com

Sleepy Pod
www.sleepypod.com

Wahl Dog Clippers
www.wahl.com

4. Memorials

Rainbow Bridge
www.rainbowbridge.com

5. Photograph front cover + some other photographs

www.K-9SuperHeroesDogWhispering.com

Published by IMB Publishing 2014

CPSIA information can be obtained at www.ICGtesting.com
Printed in the USA
BVOW06s0103051115

425627BV00007B/119/P